SNIPER ON THE EASTERN FRONT

SNIPER ON THE EASTERN FRONT

THE MEMOIRS OF SEPP ALLERBERGER KNIGHTS CROSS

Albercht Wacker

Pen & Sword
MILITARY

First published in Great Britain in 2005
and reprinted in this format in 2006, 2007, 2008,
2009, 2010, 2012, 2013, 2014, 2015 and 2016 by
PEN & SWORD MILITARY
An imprint of
Pen & Sword Books Ltd
47 Church Street
Barnsley, South Yorkshire
S70 2AS

ISBN 978 1 78159 004 1

A CIP catalogue record for this book is
available from the British Library

Printed and bound in England
By CPI Group (UK) Ltd, Croydon, CR0 4YY

Pen & Sword Books Ltd incorporates the Imprints of Aviation, Atlas,
Family History, Fiction, Maritime, Military, Discovery, Politics, History,
Archaeology, Select, Wharncliffe Local History, Wharncliffe True Crime,
Military Classics, Wharncliffe Transport, Leo Cooper, The Praetorian Press,
Remember When, Seaforth Publishing and Frontline Publishing.

For a complete list of Pen & Sword titles please contact
PEN & SWORD BOOKS LIMITED
47 Church Street, Barnsley, South Yorkshire, S70 2AS, England
E-mail: enquiries@pen-and-sword.co.uk
Website: www.pen-and-sword.co.uk

Contents

The route followed by Josef 'Sepp' Allerberger from the battle of Redkina Gap near Voroshilovsk, July 1943

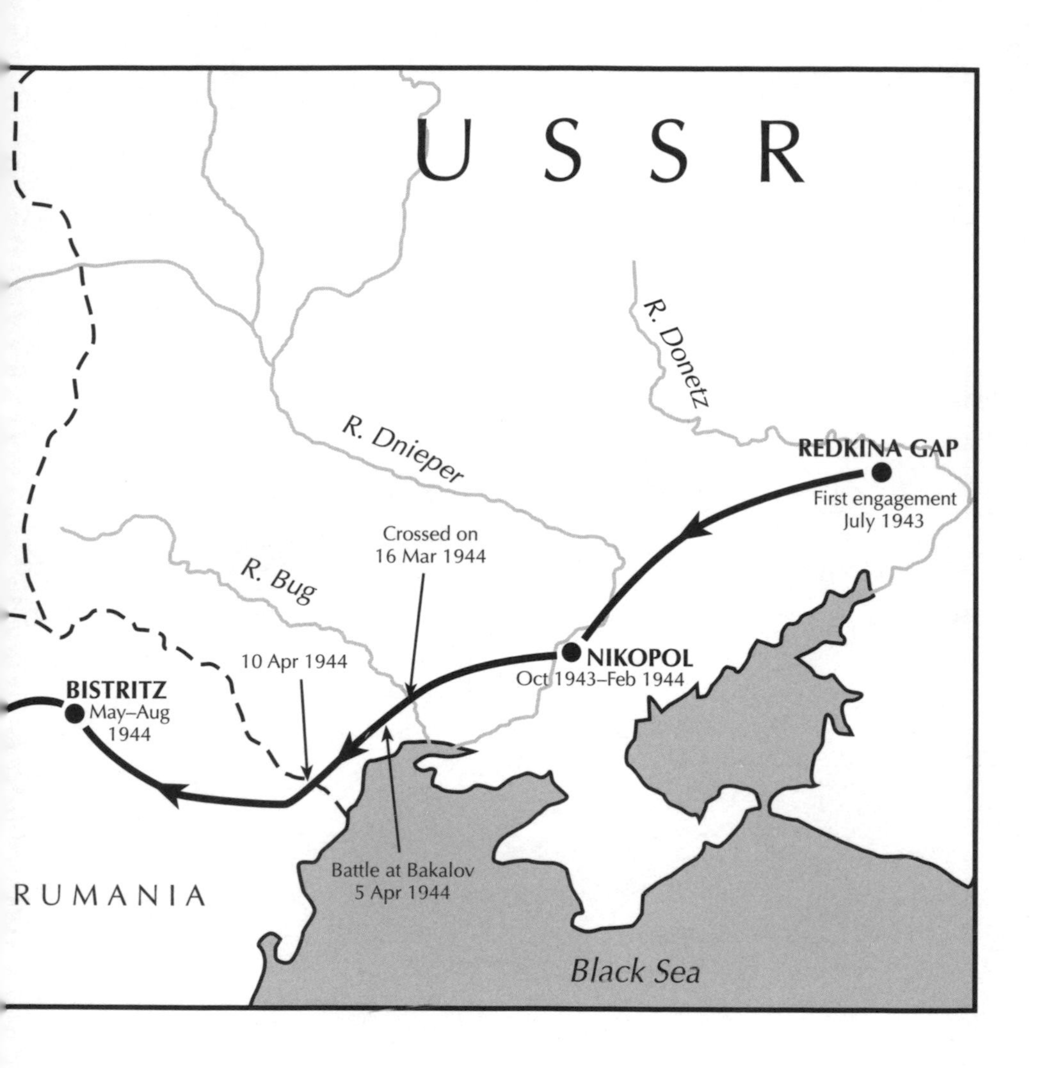
USSR
R. Donetz
R. Dnieper
R. Bug
REDKINA GAP
First engagement
July 1943
Crossed on
16 Mar 1944
NIKOPOL
Oct 1943–Feb 1944
10 Apr 1944
BISTRITZ
May–Aug
1944
Battle at Bakalov
5 Apr 1944
RUMANIA
Black Sea

Prologue

With the fall of Stalingrad there began a two-year retreat that drew the soldiers of both sides into a vortex of inhuman strain and conflict. During these two years the Eastern Front became symbolic of the German soldier's nature and the scene of uncounted human tragedies.

A great deal has been written about this war, analyzing, examining, and reporting. But finding suitable words to describe the indescribable, the daily struggle for survival, the horror and the fear, is hardly possible, and if one is to succeed at all in conveying any of this it is only achieved by concentrating on the fate of a single individual. In addition it is hard to steer a course between the rational, distanced language and contemplation of a military historian and the sympathetic approach of a biographer interested in the human dimensions of his subject.

At this book's heart stands a so-called 'sniper', exemplary of a type of soldier who, regarded with a mixture of admiration and abhorrence, is often overlooked and forgotten amid the historiography of war, yet who achieved outstanding feats and often saved the lives of many of their comrades by their courage and personal bravery, by taking an enemy's life with a precision that was sometimes terrifying. Like few other soldiers, after the war they had to live with the knowledge of having extinguished so many lives, not anonymously, but at a personal, one-to-one level, looking straight into the eye of their opponents. Nearly all of them shut this knowledge up within themselves for the rest of their lives. Hardly any of them are prepared to talk about their experiences.

After fifty years one of the best has broken his silence and, in long conversations with his biographer, has told his own story of the war. As a memento of a specialized facet of military service it provides a reminder of the real face of war, of how it looks to an infantry soldier fighting at the front.

After the passage of so many years it is inevitable that many of his memories had become blurred and that only his most traumatic experiences had remained crystal clear in his mind, and the biographer was left to join up these pieces of information and to sort them into a coherent and readable narrative. Doing so it was essential to fill the gaps in his story through thorough research, to complement and to complete it.

One other problem revealed itself to the biographer as he worked, which is expressed perfectly in the German saying 'he who wins is right, but he who loses is wrong'. While Russian and Allied marksmen are honoured as heroes, German marksmen – even in their own country – are considered as wicked killers. Because of this, it has proved necessary to protect the subject of this study by keeping his identity anonymous. Many of the names in this book are likewise fictitious, but the story is real.

The subject of this book we will call 'Sepp Allerberger'.

Sepp Allerberger was a journeyman carpenter from a little village near Salzburg, who was drawn into the growing vortex of events on the Eastern Front in the first days of July 1943. Thereafter, until the end of the war in May 1945, his life would centre around his comrades of II Battalion, Gebirgsjäger Regiment 144 (GJR 144) of 3 Gebirgsjäger Division (3 GD). The soldiers of this formation came mainly from the Alpine region. This ethnic unity was doubtless one of the main reasons for its high morale, as demonstrated throughout this story.

An Arctic winter had struck the soldiers of the Eastern Front with its icy hand. Cold, physically emaciated, and without hope, tens of thousands of men of the German Sixth Army in Stalingrad had been sacrificed, for reasons which remain dubious to this day. The fall of this city marked the obvious turning point in the fate of the Wehrmacht, which had been largely successful until then. The offensive that had led to this catastrophe was executed with energy but insufficient planning, and the conflict would now turn irrevocably into a defensive war that would end in utter chaos, with the red flag of the Soviet army flying from the roof of the Reichstag as a foretaste of the coming fifty-year partition of the nation. Germany would experience its own judgement day amid the ruins of its cities and cultural assets.

3 Gebirgsjäger Division, which will be the focus of this work, was fighting south of Stalingrad in the winter of 1942–43. With the annihilation of the Sixth Army it found itself caught up in the ensuing

Russian winter offensive. Confronted by numerically superior forces, it was only by a supreme effort and after suffering indescribable losses in men and material that the division managed to escape encirclement and thereby avoid the fate of its comrades in Stalingrad. After a murderous winter fight in the basin of Millerowo and the breakout to link up with the new defensive line in Woroschilowsk, GJR 144 was reduced to a quarter of its regular fighting strength.

Near Voroshilovsk the regiment took a firm stand, and it was built back up to strength with new recruits and equipment over the following six months.

Compared to the battles it had gone through during the winter the 144th had to deal with no more than light skirmishes and decoy attacks here. Apart from these, its war became one of combat patrols, occasional artillery barrages, and the constant threat of Russian snipers, whose victims were found mostly among the regiment's new and inexperienced recruits. Because of their lack of heavy infantry weapons the Germans were more or less helpless in the face of this phenomenon. Only in a handful of cases were they able to locate the position of a Russian sniper and shoot at him with medium infantry weapons such as mortars, machine guns and light Pak guns.

It was obvious that they were in need of marksmen of their own.

Chapter 1

The end of human innocence

A shining summer morning on the Eastern Front is just warming up. The dampness of the night gives a spicy scent of earth and grass to the warming air. But he doesn't pay any attention to Nature; he cannot let it distract him now. All his senses are tensed. He resembles a predator searching for prey. Looking through the binoculars, he scans the approaches of the Russian front line again. Somewhere out there was his enemy's perfectly disguised position, the Russian sniper who'd killed nine comrades in the last few days. He had to be an expert, because Sepp had already been searching in vain for his position for two days. But when the marksman's bullet had hit the ninth rifleman in the early hours of the morning Sepp believed he'd been able to distinguish the approximate direction from which the shot had come.

There, finally, a revealing sign. Tufts of grass standing somehow strangely below the edge of a bush. His gaze concentrated piercingly on the suspicious spot. Yes, that was exactly where he was. The adrenaline coursed through Sepp as he recognized shadowy parts of a telescopic sight, and the weapon's muzzle as it suddenly flashed. With a crashing bang he could see the projectile racing towards him. As if paralyzed, he lay there unable to escape. With a damp shock the missile hit the middle of his forehead and his head and thoughts exploded in a flash of light.

At that very moment Sepp wakes up – from a deep dream. His heart is pounding up into his throat. It feels like minutes before he can drag himself back from 1944 to the reality of the present day. Slowly he pulls himself together, but he doesn't even think of sleep any more. Through the open window of his bedroom come the muffled sounds of night and the lovely fresh air of early summer. He stands up and goes to the window. He sucks the night air deep into his tight chest.

After a few breaths his gaze settles on the silhouette of the Salzburger Alps, above which a beautiful moon is hanging. Just as clear as the moon had hung above the Russian steppe in late summer, as a tiny train with supplies for the front roared across the huge expanse. He remembered sitting in the open door of the carriage, his thoughts full of tense impatience for his coming soldier's life. 'We were poor, thoughtless small fry,' he reflects, and his thoughts began wandering. And as they had many times before over the years, episodes of his wartime life involuntarily wander through his mind. Some of the events that occurred more than fifty years ago are as fresh as if they were yesterday.

Born the son of a carpenter in September 1924, Sepp grew up in the surroundings of a village in the Salzburgerland. He spent a carefree youth guided by conservative values such as patriotism, diligence, discharge of duty, and obedience to social authorities. It was his firm anchoring in these ethical values that enabled him to accept his coming fate with such fatalism. He naturally followed in his father's footsteps and learned the carpenter's trade in preparation for taking over the family business one day. The prospect of military service he regarded as a duty and an honour at the same time, as soldiers enjoyed considerable respect in the community. Conscription was an exciting experience for young men, providing them with new self-esteem and the sense of having achieved adulthood. Sepp was a product of the social and political conditions of his time. His childhood was influenced and controlled by the dirigisme and strong ideological policies of the Third Reich, which was practised at linking national self-consciousness and conservative virtues with unquestioning readiness for duty, especially among the young, in order to implement its political aims. It was natural for young men of Sepp's age to report to the Wehrmacht voluntarily, to fulfil the aspirations of their government by force of arms.

After almost three years of war, with the Wehrmacht marching from one victorious campaign to the next, many young men were almost afraid of missing their chance to participate in the fighting, because according to the omnipresent propaganda machine final victory was now in sight. Distanced from the bitter and merciless reality of war, the day when they were declared fit for military service in the autumn of 1942 was one of honour for the village's young men. The mayor gave a short speech about service to the Fatherland and the heroic struggle against Bolshevism. The fire brigade orchestra serenaded them merrily, and some girls of the *Bund Deutscher Mädchen* (League of German Maidens) pinned little bouquets to the lapels of the future heroes. The thought of possible death or mutilation didn't occur to anyone, but six of the young men who proudly posed for a group portrait would not survive the next two years. A few months later they reported for duty filled with high hopes.

After finishing his apprenticeship aged 18 in February 1943, Sepp, like nearly all the young men from his region, was called up to serve in the Gebirgsjäger (mountain troops), based at Kufstein in the Tyrol. After being kitted out, he and his comrades were transferred to Mittenwald for their infantry basic training ten days later. After six months of being driven hard Sepp was a machine gunner. During the whole of his training period the topic of 'snipers' as a tactical aspect of infantry combat was not mentioned at all. There were just some derogatory remarks about Russian snipers and women with shotguns, who were to be fought by the machine gunners vigorously and relentlessly. The training was hard, but without the harassment evident in the peacetime army or in the early stages of the war. Instead it concentrated on preparing the young men – at least physically – for the hardship they would face in the field, and on familiarizing them with their weapons. In particular the instructors, who had experience of fighting at the front, tried to pass on their knowledge. They knew about the dramatically high losses suffered among new soldiers sent to the front as replacements, who were overwhelmed by the horrifying reality of war. Exposed suddenly to the merciless brutality of combat, many were seized with primeval panic and an uncontrollable desire to flee. But though this behaviour might have saved them in olden times, in an age of sophisticated weapons of war capable of killing over great distances it led to their downfall.

Careful training could prepare an individual for the moment of confrontation, but it could do little to help control the natural instinct to run away from danger. In the last resort everybody has to decide for himself – and then not until the moment of conflict actually arrives – if he can look calmly into war's countenance or not. It is at that moment that the warrior emerges, to whom fighting is second nature and the battlefield is home, but who is forever confronted by the eternal quandary of 'kill or be killed'. Only from such a forge of warlike reality does a sniper emerge, a soldier who knows how to keep his mind clear, who is able to act in the front line in the heat of battle, and who knows how to apply his weapon, the rifle with its telescopic sight, to optimum effect. Only these soldiers deserve the name 'marksmen'.

At the beginning of September 1942, Sepp and his comrades got their marching orders to join GJR 144, which was still in the southern part of the Eastern Front, near Voroshilovsk. They were among the final batch of replacements sent to bring the regiment up to its full fighting strength. But before this they received a three-day pass, though the three days passed like the batting of an eyelid. For most of them it was the last opportunity in their young lives to see their families and to say farewell. The uncertainty of his future was indescribable, but Sepp's mother stroked his head at every opportunity and tried to caress him. His father, a soldier in the First World War, hid his concern in silence and hard work. The inescapable day of separation arrived. When Sepp got on the bus that would take him back to the barracks at Mittenwald, his mother was all tears. His father embraced him when saying goodbye, which he didn't normally do, and, obviously trying to maintain his composure, whispered into his ear: 'Take care of yourself, boy. It's my dearest wish that you return unharmed. But it's in God's hands.' When the bus started, Sepp waved briefly just once, and then faced forward suddenly with a fixed expression. Otherwise he would have lost the composure that he had only managed to maintain with difficulty.

It was anxiously observed that in the area of 3 Gebirgsjäger Division the Red Army was preparing for a major offensive to the Donezbecken (the Donets Basin) and the Ukraine, strengthened by the arrival of supplies of new American weapons. Every man who increased the fighting strength of the German units was therefore highly welcome. Sepp and his companions travelled across the infinite Russian steppe for days in straw-strewn cattle wagons before they reached their destination, the Donezbecken. Their arrival in Voroshilovsk coincided with the very beginning of the Russian attack. Without any chance of becoming acclimatized to life at the front, the day after their arrival they were thrown into the battle for the Redkinaschlucht, which was extraordinarily hard and resulted in many losses. In the opinion of the average 'Landser', or common soldier, Sepp had a really hard lot, because 3 GD would serve in an atypical, purely infantry role in the southern sector of the Eastern Front for the rest of the war, always at the heart of the fighting. The unit's losses were consequently enormous and proportionately far higher than in the rest of the army.

With its extensive coalmines the Donezbecken was an important source of raw materials, so it was of the highest importance to both parties. The mines, with their huge tunnel systems, had not been entirely cleared of enemy troops when the Germans advanced. Entire Russian units just let the Wehrmacht roll past them as they hid in the tunnels and then emerged in the midst of the surprised Landsers. As a result there were murderous close-quarter combats that extended even into the tunnel system itself.

The Soviets had already broken through the German lines in an energetic attack before Sepp reached the front, and now they tried to extend this bridgehead. The commander of 3 GD estimated the situation as very precarious, so he made a counterstrike without any further preparations or regrouping of his forces. This succeeded, but it was a victory bought by huge losses among the Landsers.

It was at daybreak on 18 July 1943 that Sepp and his fellow riflemen finally arrived and went quietly to their quarters. Their thoughts were turned inwards and worry and nervousness were written on their faces. Everyone had his own method of coping with the fear that came before deployment. The experienced men were chewing crusts of bread with a dark expression on their faces, or were smoking, or just pulled themselves together with expressionless faces. The newer ones had huge difficulty controlling their nervousness; they were uneasy, restless, twitchy. Many were puking, and they crapped and pissed continually. Lacking any experience of what was about to come, Sepp took the strange scene in with a distinct sense of dread. He was unable to eat, his stomach was about to rebel, and his body felt like jelly. He felt as if he couldn't move. In this critical situation he was lucky, because his section leader was very experienced, and despite being battle-hardened remained sensitive to the needs of the new men in his unit. He recognized Sepp's fear and talked to him reassuringly: 'Breathe deeply, man. Just think of your machine gun and shoot like you've learned to. Pay attention to me and to my orders. I take care of my boys, and if it's really hard I'm with you. Up to now I've brought my unit out of every mess and nobody will be left behind.' A mixture of juvenile naivety and trust in the character of his group leader gave Sepp the necessary strength to overcome his anxiety and confront the events that would accompany his baptism of fire.

It was almost 05:00 when the attack began with a barrage of artillery fire from their rear. With dull thuds, the earth was torn apart in front of the riflemen and soil was blown into the clear morning sky in huge fountains. The totally new sounds felt uncomfortable in Sepp's ears, where they mixed with the roar of bullet impacts and the high buzz of pieces of shrapnel. He and the other riflemen crouched in their positions and waited for the order to attack. After about twenty minutes the artillery fire broke off and suddenly Sepp recognized an unusual sound. It was the animal sound of wounded Russians. The order to attack came amid the horror that was beginning to grow inside him. All the tension and nervousness was suddenly released into movement. Like a vortex, the violent commencement of the battle dragged the Landsers away with it. Suddenly Russian grenades were exploding in the riflemen's lines. As Sepp jumped up there was a buzzing, tearing sound. To his right a comrade, a young guy of his own age from Berchtesgarden, was staring incredulously at his torn uniform jacket, from which his intestines were pouring out, more and more of them with every movement. After a few seconds of shock he started to scream tremendously and tried to stuff the steaming intestines back inside. Sepp wanted to help him and he put down his MG, but his section leader hit him on the back and screamed: 'Come on, attack, nobody can help him, give covering fire to your comrades!' As Sepp broke free of his paralysis the wounded man suddenly went silent and, with a mystified look in his eyes, sank to his knees and tipped over face down on the earth. Sepp, who was already 20m away, did not see the releasing death of his comrade. His thoughts were wiped away, and he was seized by a primitive will to survive. Death, injury and fear were meaningless. His entire existence was reduced to shooting, loading, jumping forward, looking for cover and peering about for the enemy, his target, like an animal. An alteration was taking place within him. In the ensuing hours of vehemently raging conflict the naive young man turned into a Landser, a warrior in the original meaning of the word. The mixture of fear, blood and death was like a drug, which was on the one hand intoxicating, but on the other depressing, because it not only marked the end of human innocence but also swept away the future and the expectation of a future life. Killing became a trade forced on him, and his fate wanted him to perfect it to mastery.

Sepp's group worked its way carefully through the bushes until it was suddenly ambushed from a distance of about 20m. A rifleman fell without a word in the hail of bullets from a volley of automatic-weapons fire. Sepp returned fire instantly, while the unhurt riflemen sought cover. Then they threw hand grenades towards the enemy position and advanced, giving covering fire to each other, only to find that the enemy had suddenly disappeared. Pushing forward into the group of bushes they found four dead Russians in front of a masterfully disguised mine entrance. The dead bodies looked totally emaciated and cadaverous. Probably they had been holding out in the tunnel for months.

There were fresh tracks leading back into the mine. A mixture of curiosity and fascination compelled some of the riflemen to go in, their weapons held ready in firing position. A few minutes after the earth had swallowed them up Sepp heard the dull sound of shots deep inside. Shortly after that the riflemen staggered back into the daylight deathly pale and obviously quite confused. There was no time to ask questions, because a Russian company was now attacking the sector and the swirl of battle drew the riflemen away.

The relentless struggle lasted until dusk at about 22:00. It was a wonder to Sepp that he had survived this day, in contrast to many of his comrades. Now his company was pulled back to the start line from which the morning's attack had commenced. Because of the underestimated resistance put up by the Russians the attack would have to be mounted anew the next day, and both sides took the opportunity to regroup. This pause in the fighting was used to see to the smaller injuries of those who remained fit for action, and to bring up supplies of food and ammunition. Sitting with a crust of bread, a can of fish and a cigarette, they talked about the most significant events of the day. This was the first opportunity for Sepp to ask his surviving comrades what had happened in the tunnel. In short sentences, still clearly shocked by the unexpected horror of what they had seen, two of the surviving riflemen described an incredible event of the sort that seemed to happen every day during this war.

Groping their way forward in the pale light of the tunnel, after about 50m the men had found a meagrely-lit cave that stank unbearably. It took them a few moments to adjust to the darkness before the horror became visible. In a corner two Russians were squatting alongside each other. Close by were the remains of two carefully preserved human bodies lying on ammunition boxes. They had obviously been smoked above the fire in order to preserve them. Next to a pile of excrement in another corner were their intestines, which were starting to decay, and gnawed bones. Shaking with disgust, one of the riflemen who was able to speak a little Russian asked the two survivors what had happened.

They reported that they had been left with thirty-five men in this tunnel when the Russians withdrew, with strict orders to stay in hiding and hold the position until their army counterattacked. This counterattack didn't come for months, so very soon all their supplies were used up. Their officer nevertheless ensured that they complied with their orders, and when many of the soldiers demanded that they should withdraw he killed the two youngest – they were just sixteen years old – as a deterrent. He shot them in the neck in cold blood, and then ordered the other soldiers at gunpoint to gut them, carve them up, and smoke their body parts over the fire. He forced the soldiers to divide the corpses' livers and to eat them fresh. For the next few weeks they lived on the offenders' flesh. They did not even think of rebelling against the officer, because their sergeant and the other two non-commissioned officers sided with him and secured all their weapons in boxes. Before long the bodies were eaten, and the officer then shot the next youngest soldier without mercy. A few days after that the Russian attack finally retook the tunnel and this obliged the group to come out.

While the rifleman translated this report, one of the other German soldiers started to puke, overwhelmed by disgust. Once he could breathe again, he shouted, 'You revolting arse-holes,' and fired his MP40. In disbelief, their eyes full of panic, the two Russians stared at the impacts on their bodies, while foaming blood came from their chapped, speechless lips. With a final twitch of their tortured bodies their lives leaked away. 'Get out of here, boys,' shouted the section leader, and they hurried out, leaving the nightmarish scene behind them. They sucked in mouthfuls of fresh air greedily.

To the experienced Landsers this was just an incident of war, but Sepp was overwhelmed by a flood of extreme emotions, gaining insight to the unplumbed depths of human experience. Yet this was no more than an almost innocuous introduction to war's depravity compared to what would follow. But this was no time for profound thoughts. Sleep and hunger were demanding attention, and there were just a few hours of rest left.

In the end it took four days before the Soviet resistance could be broken with the support of additional artillery and assault weapons. This tongue of conquered Russian soil was bought with the lives of 650 German soldiers.

At the end of the five days Sepp had lost even the last shreds of his juvenile naivety. The experience of these murderous battles had already etched its lines into his face, making him look ten years older. His company, the 7th, had been reduced to just twenty men. Of his own squad only he and his section leader were left. Sepp had lost all sensation of time, fear and compassion. He was a product of the events around him, driven by a primitive instinct to survive the demands of combat, hunger, thirst and exhaustion.

Chapter 2

'Try your luck as a sniper'

On 22 July the struggle to restore the former German front line succeeded. The Russians fought with desperate courage. Well camouflaged, they often demonstrated enormous fire discipline, only shooting from a distance of under 50m. This way nearly every shot hit its target. The Russian marksmen in particular made sure that the German riflemen were cut to the quick.

The realization dawned on Machine Gunner Allerberger that his job was a suicide mission more than anything else. The strategic importance of machine guns inevitably meant that they drew the energetic fire of heavy weapons such as mortars and infantry guns, and – especially in mobile battles – snipers. As a result the losses among machine gunners were disproportionately high. It therefore became clear to him even after the first few days that his chances of survival depended urgently upon finding himself another role within the company.

It was just a dull hit against his left hand, when the piece of shrapnel hit Sepp on his fifth day of battle. He accepted the injury with an amazingly cool fatalism, as an inevitable consequence of war. Astonishingly it did not hurt and it hardly bled. He checked the flexibility of his hand and was reassured that it seemed unaffected. He dropped behind with his MG, ripped up a set of bandages, and with the help of his comrade bandaged the gaping wound at the base of his thumb. He barely had the bandage on before his companion shouted: 'Seppi, look out – they're coming. Shoot, shoot!'

An hour later, when the company was pulled out of the fighting line and he got a little rest, he finally felt the pain. At the assembly point, which was also the supply depot, a doctor with a few ambulance men was giving first aid to the wounded, and Sepp went to have his own wound treated. A small farmhouse with a thatched roof, a little way from the regiment's headquarters, housed the makeshift hospital. Without feeling any emotion Sepp listened to the moaning, whimpering cries and breathed in the aroma of raw flesh. One of the medics was sorting the incoming casualties according to the seriousness of their wounds. A very young soldier was brought in carried on a square of tent cloth. Below his boyish face, which was moaning stereotypically 'I can't move, oh God I can't move,' his motionless body dangled like a marionette. The medical sergeant lifted the wounded man and examined his chest, which was unhurt from the front. But between his shoulder blades there was a gaping hole as big as two hands. Emerging from this were bone fragments from his ribs and spine. Carefully he laid him back into the tent square. 'We can't help this one, boys. With this wound death is a mercy. Bring him over to the barn to the priest.' All the hopeless cases were being sent to the barn, where a chaplain – obviously overwhelmed by grief – was trying to give the mortally wounded what little comfort he could.

Sepp's wound was judged as a trifle, so he had to wait in a queue to see a medical sergeant, who was cleaning and stitching flesh wounds with practised expertise. There was a sergeant sitting next to Sepp whose right forearm was bound with a handkerchief tourniquet tightened by a stick: his nearly severed hand was dangling from a last few tendons as if from strings. He stared unmovingly at the floor in a state of shock.

It was three more hours before it was finally Sepp's turn. Without a word the sergeant removed the bandage, examined the wound for possible foreign bodies, and then cleaned it with a solution of Sulfonamit. A very strong medical lance-corporal then grabbed Sepp's arm and turned his back towards him so that his view of the wound was blocked. As soon as he had done so the sergeant started, without anaesthetic, to quickly and skilfully cut the wound's edges clean and to stitch it. Holding his arm in an iron grip, the lance-corporal said: 'Cry out if you want, it will take your mind off it.' Sepp felt his self-control failing, and he became fully conscious of the pain. His screams expressed the inhuman experiences of the last few days.

His wound required rest, so he was transferred to the regimental transport troop for fourteen days along with some comrades who had also been slightly wounded, in order to do light auxiliary work. During this time the regiment, which had been bled white, was transferred back to Voroshilovsk to await reinforcements of personnel and material. Sepp, who you'll remember was a carpenter, was assigned to the regiment's Weaponry NCO as an assistant and given the task of sorting the captured weapons and, as his recovery progressed, of repairing the stocks of damaged German carbines.

It was here in the relative safety of the regimental headquarters that Sepp, after reflecting on his situation, determined that he would try to escape further duty as a machine gunner at the first opportunity.

It was perhaps an omen that he found a single Russian sniper rifle amongst the weapons he had to sort. Immediately he saw it Sepp asked the Weaponry NCO if he could have this gun for practising. They had enough Russian ammunition, and, in a clairvoyant moment, the Weaponry NCO said to him: 'Show me what you can do. Perhaps you're born to be a sniper. We need such boys to give Ivan a good going over. You know how his marksmen make our lives miserable.'

That same evening Sepp started practising. After a few days it became apparent that he had the right touch for accurate shooting, and the Weaponry NCO was impressed by his shooting skills. Seemingly without any effort he could hit a matchbox from 100m, and from 300m could hit a wooden ammunition box measuring about 30 by 30cm.

The fourteen days of rest passed quickly, the wound was healing, and Sepp had to get back to his company. When he said goodbye to the Weaponry NCO the latter handed him the gun with its telescopic sight. 'Sepp, I talked to your old man,' this being the name used by Landsers for their company commander. 'He doesn't mind if you try your luck as a sniper. Come on boy, show Ivan!'

In the first days of August 1943 Sepp arrived back at his company with the sniper rifle under his arm. When he reported to his sergeant he informally received the black 'wounded in action' medal with a certificate. 'Allerberger, don't you think that it's all over after that. That was just a foretaste. Keep your arse close to the turf, all the more now that you're a sniper. Now go and give Ivan a good going over.'

The front was relatively quiet and the fighting was restricted to minor artillery duels and skirmishes between patrols. But the pressure was enormous because of the Russian marksmen. It was extremely dangerous to expose oneself, and in spite of the Germans' general caution the Russians found their mark again and again. In his commanding officer Sepp had an open-minded superior who knew the advantages of marksmen and who lamented their absence in the German army. This viewpoint was not widespread. Many officers regarded snipers as dishonourable and perfidious fighters, and refused to use them. An officer of 3 GD expressed this attitude quite vividly in his memoirs: 'Perhaps he was one of those gunmen who crawled outside in the dawn or before dusk and who were lying still, with a view – like a cat above a mouse-hole – through their telescopic sight of the hostile gunman's position, from which a shoulder or a head was lifting – just for a moment – but just enough. And a shot shattered the silence. From a slowly cramping hand an empty tin is falling. The urge that cost him his life. That is War!' (An explanation about that: one problem for soldiers stuck in trenches is that they have to answer the call of nature. For hygienic reasons they can't fill the trench with excrement, so after a few days at the front Landsers learnt to use empty tins as camp toilets. After they'd relieved themselves, the smell and the grumbling of their comrades necessitated swift disposal of the contents, and it was when swinging the tin over the lip of the trench that inexperienced soldiers sometimes rose too high, for fear of making a mess. A good sniper would use such opportunities for a clear shot without any remorse.)

But in the end such officers' comments were self-righteousness. War is not ethical and not heroic. Its object is to achieve a political aim through the use of maximum violence, and the price is death, mutilation and destruction. It makes absolutely no difference if you're hit by the bullet of a sniper or torn apart by a mortar shell. And if the fragile question of honour is the point at issue, who is the more honest and brave in a fight, the officer who, for example, sends an entire company to be slaughtered to achieve some strategic aim, for personal glory, or as a result of tactical incompetence, or the 'perfidious' but highly effective sniper who continually exposes himself to considerable risk?

Anyway, Sepp had escaped his suicidal role as a machine gunner. Now he was directly under the company commander. Because the military situation was largely limited to defending their own positions at this time, his commander allowed the new sniper to hunt within the bounds of the company area. Instinctively Sepp set about things the right way, and went around the trenches to ask his comrades what they had seen. He was welcomed with a sigh of relief: 'Finally we have a sniper – show them, Sepp!' A machine-gun group leader took him by his jacket sleeve and pulled him into a sap. Through a hole between the tree trunks that were piled along the trench's edge as protection, he showed him the Russian positions and explained: 'Over there is a sniper. He shoots at everything. Look here, even the crockery that we held above the trench has got a hole in it. Can you get rid of him?'

Chapter 3

An unfathomable and essential share of luck

Straining his eyes, Sepp peered through the small hole between the tree trunks with the 8x magnification binoculars he'd been given at the instigation of the company quartermaster sergeant, but he couldn't see anything suspicious. After that he suggested carefully holding a rolled tent square with a cap on it above the edge of the trench, while he observed the Russian position. The Russian marksman seemed to be quite inexperienced, because as soon as the cap was showing above the trench's edge he fired. Sepp saw the muzzle flash of his opponent flicker from a pile of wood like a breath of wind. Now that he knew where the Russian was concealed he could even make out his telescopic sight by a slight shimmer on the lens. Already in this first deployment Sepp was demonstrating an intuitive feel for his new role as a marksman, because unlike his opponent he understood the first rule of survival: never shoot at a target you haven't certainly identified. Shoot only once from one position, then immediately either change position or become invisible within it.

His counterpart stayed in his position and was waiting for a new target – a fatal mistake which he was about to pay for with his life. Sepp laid out a rolled tent square behind the tree trunks as a support and carefully pushed the muzzle of his gun through the gap. He was unable to use his telescopic sight because the opening was not big enough, but the Russian was lying only about 90m away, so he could aim the regular way using the fore and rear sights.

Suddenly he became nervous. His comrades were expecting an absolutely precise shot, and he abruptly realized he had the task of killing a man in calculated and pre-meditated cold blood for the first time in his life. Scruples gnawed at his conscience. His throat went dry, his heart was racing, and his hands trembled. He felt paralyzed and was unable to pull the trigger, and he had to put his rifle down and take deep breaths to regain his composure. His comrades were standing around and staring at him, full of expectation. Repeatedly he raised his weapon into a firing position, adjusted it carefully, and then hesitated again. 'Well, what now? Give him a wallop,' he heard a comrade saying as if from far away. And suddenly the strain left him. As if in a dream, with machine-like precision his trigger finger started to move. He took the pressure point, breathed deeply in and out, held his breath and pulled the trigger. The shot rang out, there was dust in front of his muzzle and he could not see. But a comrade who was looking through another hole between the logs was shouting: 'You got him, lad! A perfect hit. That swine is dead.' Like a brushfire the news sped through the trenches: the Russian marksman had been finished off.

Suddenly machine guns started to shoot, carbines crashed, and somebody shouted 'Attack!' Astonished by this activity and the unexpected German assault the Russians hurried from their advance trenches and fled back to their main fighting line. Meeting no resistance the German riflemen stormed into the abandoned positions, Sepp among them. He and those who had witnessed his first shot as a marksman were curious to see its results, and they ran over to the woodpile behind which their opponent had been lying. He had dug a trench-like hollow in which his lifeless body was now lying. Only the feet were visible. Next to them there was a seeping trickle of blood. Grabbing his ankles two riflemen pulled him out so that the extent of his deadly wound could be seen. A bloody mess of brain and bone splinters was covering his back. In the back of his head there was a gaping hole as big as a fist so that they could see the inside of his skull, which had been cleared out by the shockwave of the bullet. The Landsers, who were accustomed to such sights, turned him on his back to reveal the face of a boy, who may have been 16 years old. Sepp's missile had hit his right eye. 'You got him neatly, lad, and you did it from a distance of nearly a hundred metres without your telescopic sight. You're really good, Sepp,' was the comment of one of the riflemen. Sepp looked down at his victim with a mixture of pride, horror, and guilt. Suddenly he felt a lump coming up his throat and he had to puke. Convulsively retching, he coughed up a mixture of bread, *Muckefuck* (a Landser nickname for malt coffee) and sardines.

Though he was embarrassed by this public display of weakness, his comrades reacted with sympathy and understanding to his supposed lack of self-control. A sergeant who was one and a half heads taller than Sepp, with a big reddish moustache and a roguishly impish twinkle in his blue eyes – he may have been ten years Sepp's senior – comforted him in a striking North German accent: 'You don't have to be ashamed, boy, this happened to every one of us. You gotta go through that. Better to puke clean than to shit in your pants. And daddy has always got some hot stuff with him just in case.' With that he pulled a silvery shining hip flask from his breast pocket and offered it to Sepp. 'Here, take a good swig. This will pull the worry lines from your balls. But don't you dribble bits of your puke into it, else I'll pull your noodle up to your top button.' Gratefully Sepp took a large gulp. When he handed the bottle back to the sergeant it shot through his mind: 'This guy looks just like a Viking, only the horns on the helmet are missing,' and he had to smile at the thought of a Viking among the mountain infantry. But there was no time for contemplation and personal feelings, because while they ransacked the abandoned Russian trenches for usable booty the Soviets counterattacked, and as fast as the Landsers had won this fight their success was melting away again. An hour later everything was as it had been, and everybody was back in his old place. But Sepp had passed his initiation test as a marksman and his comrades were spreading the story of his success in all directions. So he got more admiration than criticism, and this helped him to overcome any lingering doubts about what he had done.

He consigned his second lesson to memory: war is a merciless process of killing and being killed. In a fight, compassion for your enemy is suicide, because every opponent you do not kill can kill you the next moment. Your chances of survival increase in proportion to your soldierly skills and your lack of sympathy for your enemy. This was a principle that he observed until the end of the war. If he had an enemy in his sights and his finger on the trigger, then his fate was sealed – without exception.

Sepp managed to shoot two more careless Russians the same day. In juvenile pride at his success he cut three notches on the stock of his gun with his penknife, a ritual that he kept up as long as he had his Russian gun with its telescopic sight. Not until a comrade tragically died a year later did he give up this suicidal habit.

The same day the sergeant told him that he had to report his hits to the company headquarters, always naming a witness of non-commissioned officer or officer rank. But the only hits that counted were those not made in an attack or in the defence of a position. He had to keep a little book listing his hits and an officer or a sergeant always had to confirm it. For every ten confirmed hits he got a silver cord 7cm long and 1cm wide, like those on the collars of sergeants, and this was sewn on his left forearm. But getting confirmation of hits was often an annoying affair. Some of his superiors envied his success and refused to give their signature. This was especially true of artillery observers, who were often young officers full of soldierly idealism who thought of their own marksmen as insidious snipers and showed their antipathy by refusing to confirm their hits. Another reason why marksmen and artillery observers didn't get along too well was the fact that marksmen used to steal the observers' superior equipment, such as jackets, blankets and tent squares. Sepp would become a master at such unofficial procurement of officers' equipment.

In the next fourteen days he was successful twenty-seven times, and his new task quickly became a routine. As a novice he nevertheless had a fair share of luck, because the Russian marksmen shunned him, not knowing of his actual inexperience. Besides, his company's part of the front stayed relatively quiet. This gave him the opportunity to learn from experience and from his mistakes, an advantage that many other novice marksmen did not have, so that they often had to pay for their mistakes with their lives.

But this quiet period was soon over. On 18 August 1943, after some days of increasing Russian pressure, there was a huge attack along the whole length of the Donets front. With an overwhelming superiority in numbers, the Russians were able to break through, and the riflemen had to abandon their positions. But now that they were on the defensive the true tactical significance of a good marksman became apparent. Although Sepp had been at the front for only a few weeks he already had the stoic resolve and coolness of an experienced Landser. Even in desperate situations he kept his nerve and fought with inspiration and luck – an ability that could not be taught, not even during the best training. Only the reality of battle showed if you were a real soldier in control of your personal fear and in possession of the natural reflexes necessary to escape.

3 Gebirgsjäger Division started its systematic withdrawal to the Dnieper. With the powerful superiority of thirty-three complete

divisions compared to just ten denuded formations on the German side, the Russians stormed the German positions, where ninety soldiers had to defend each kilometre of front line. Gaps were plugged by deploying second-line and logistical troops. So there was no staggering of units, and no reserves. A Soviet breakthrough would therefore have immediate and highly dangerous consequences.

3 GD was at the centre of the heaviest fighting near Zaporizhzya, where two Russian wedges were trying to break through and close a pincer movement. Although the riflemen of GJR 144 were in a strategically important position facing an enemy ten times their strength, their line held, enabling the other units to withdraw in good order and construct a new defensive line. At the beginning of September the roads were turned into a knee-deep morass by the continuous rain of an early autumn. Constant lack of sleep, problems in the supply of food and ammunition, and the unremitting pressure of fighting were using up the last reserves of the riflemen's stamina – a situation that would become typical of the rest of the war.

Sepp's company was ordered to cover the retreat of the regiment. Its sixty riflemen were positioned in a village around a strategically important crossroads, to keep the Russians' mechanized advance troops busy. The enemy's reconnaissance established the company's numerical inferiority quite quickly and more Russian units were sent up to annihilate them. The remaining men of 7 Company were experienced soldiers, and being well entrenched and capable of laying down accurate fire they managed to keep the Russians at a good distance. They even endured the fire of small artillery weapons and tanks with few losses. It was in battles like these that marksmen proved their worth. Shot after shot, Sepp would hit his target at distances of up to 300m, forcing the enemy to seek cover from the deadly accuracy of his almost unerring aim. In such desperate fights it was a decisive advantage if you could shake the enemy's morale. An experienced marksman didn't necessarily want to kill his victims outright, but rather to put shots into the torso, which were as painful as possible and put him out of action. Besides enabling the marksman to achieve a higher quota of hits during the mad rush of the fighting, the animal-like screams of heavily wounded men demoralized their comrades and broke up the momentum of an attack. It was in these battles, against superior numbers mounting mass attacks, that Sepp developed a personal tactic to perfection. He would ignore the first three or four lines of attackers and then pump as many rounds as possible into the stomachs of men in the hindmost wave. Their startled cries of pain, and the fact that they came from behind, unnerved the front ranks, and the attack started to falter. That was the moment when Sepp would switch his attention to the foremost attackers. Enemies nearer than 50m he would bring down with fatal head or heart shots, as far as possible, to put them out of action instantly. Enemies further away than 50m were shot in the torso instead, to wound as many of them as possible. With fleeing enemies especially, shots into the kidneys were effective, leading to the wounded men screaming inhumanly. As a result the attack would often break off suddenly. In situations like these Sepp might achieve more than twenty hits in as few minutes, though these didn't count towards his score.

For two days he helped to ensure the survival of the little unit in this way. But to escape the inevitability of annihilation they had to withdraw, since their strength was shrinking continuously. During the second night 7 Company managed to make off through a breach they had created in the dusk, taking thirteen wounded with them. Again it was the marksman who held their pursuers at a respectable distance, until they reached their own new fighting line at dawn. Of course, the question of ethics and soldierly honour during such a fight doubtless rears its head to modern readers. But in the midst of uncontrolled violence personal survival and the survival of one's comrades are the only guidelines to how one should act.

Even after they had reached the main fighting line there was no time to think of well-earned rest. As the new day dawned the Russians attacked again, more cautiously, but it still demanded all their attention. This time three tanks were rattling along ahead of the advancing riflemen. Sepp had created a well-concealed position for himself among his comrades, where he hoped to stay undiscovered for a long time. The Landsers had disguised all of their new entrenchments as well as they could, to take the Russians as much by surprise as possible. Accordingly the enemy was approaching carefully, being uncertain of what he faced.

The Soviet infantry were sheltering behind their slowly moving tanks, which were now about 150m from the German positions. With a jerk the front tank stopped, its turret turning with a buzzing sound to aim its cannon towards the German lines without having actually located them. The turret stopped, and a few seconds later the hatch opened. Sepp already had his gun in firing position, its telescopic sight focused on the cover. Carefully a head emerged through the opening, which was about two hands wide, and lifted a pair of binoculars to its eyes. Sepp's rifle was ranged to about 120m at this point, so he calculated that if he aimed a few centimetres higher his shot should hit the tankman's head. A direct hit was his duty in such a situation, because the report of his rifle would be the signal for the battle to begin. Sepp hesitated for a few seconds, and then the thought came into his mind that this might be the commander of the tanks and perhaps of the whole attack. His death might decide the entire battle. A deep breath, a moment of concentration, then the quiet and steady pressure of his finger on the trigger and the bark of the rifle. Through his telescopic sight Sepp saw a splash of blood hit the hatch, and the head disappeared inside the tank. Seconds later the fight was raging. But the tanks didn't move. They just shot towards the German lines without harming them. After a few minutes their motors started to roar, and the three colossi of steel withdrew. Sepp's guess had obviously been correct. The Russian attack was clearly leaderless, and when the enemy tried again after about an hour their attack did not have the necessary pace and determination. A single well-aimed shot had resulted in the demoralization of the enemy, and had, in all probability, enabled the riflemen to stand firm.

On 20 September the offensive ended. The German front, which had shortened in the meantime, had been scantily strengthened, and thanks to the high morale of 3 Gebirgsjäger Division an enemy breakthrough had been prevented. On the other hand GJR 144 had lost more than half of its soldiers. Those who remained were drained, dirty, lousy, wounded and ill, their faces etched with deep lines resulting from the superhuman strain of their ordeal. The Nazi propaganda machine cynically described these faces as 'the heroic physiognomy of warriors on the Eastern Front, forged in the fire of combat'.

Sepp, amazingly, had got through it all without a scratch, though he suffered from lice (lovingly called *Sackratten* by the Landsers) and diarrhoea, resulting from the fact that, like many of his comrades, he had lived for days on salty cucumbers found in the pantries of deserted Russian farmhouses.

The division used the temporary lull in the fighting to build a new defence line, the Wotanstellung. In their present location the Landsers got a peculiar feeling of being at home, because they were in the area settled by Volga-Germans, who had been deported here by the Russians long before. Amid the neat little villages and small towns with names like Heidelberg, Tiefenbrunn and Rosenberg – their houses neat and tidy with the crockery in the cupboards, looking as if their owners would return at any moment – the Germans constructed their entrenchments, knowing that within a few days or perhaps weeks the storm of war would sweep over them. Strange feelings of their own homes being under a similar threat crept into the soldiers, an omen of things to come.

While the Red Army was gathering itself for a new offensive, GJR 144 received inadequate reinforcement in the form of men returning from leave or hospital. The supplies of weapons and ammunition they received were not as much as they expected either. The most important tasks were to ensure that the regimental area was thoroughly cleared of the enemy, to accurately anticipate the enemy's next point of attack, and to distribute their own very limited forces correctly. It was important to mislead the enemy concerning their strength by mounting bold patrols. During the early hours of morning and in the evening Sepp stalked beyond the German lines, to clear out and discourage careless Russian patrols, surprising and decimating them with his well-aimed fire and driving the survivors back to their own positions unnerved. Patrols did not expect a confrontation with a single marksman so far in front of the lines, and such contacts hit the patrols of both sides like a bolt out of the blue. That is why Sepp often managed to shoot several members of a patrol before they could find cover or withdraw to a safe distance.

In the dawn of a wonderful autumn morning in late September, Sepp was lying well disguised on the top of a small hill that was covered with trees. He was observing a Russian artillery position about a thousand metres away when suddenly a Russian patrol emerged cautiously from a copse about 150m in front of him. Led by a very young lieutenant, the obviously careless group appeared in the early morning sun in single file, much too close together. With practised self-control in order not to reveal his position, Sepp brought his gun carefully into firing position and was amazed as he watched the inexperienced procedure of the patrol. As usual, he first took the officer into the reticle of his telescopic sight, and was fascinated to see that he seemed to be a member of the Russian political top brass. It was highly unusual, but he wore a custom-made uniform of refined cloth and wonderful boots of the best leather. Spellbound, watching the scene with his finger ready on the trigger, Sepp saw the lieutenant stumble over a tree root. Relaxing his finger, he saw the Russian get up and pull a snow-white handkerchief with a crocheted edge from his pocket to clean his fingers and his uniform. To Sepp, living with dirt, smell, vermin, and the daily ruthless fight for survival, the incongruity of the scene inspired mixed emotions of absurdity and a yearning for more tranquil times. But war leaves no room for sentimentality. Sparing this patrol would have put himself and his comrades in immediate danger. While he was looking through his telescopic sight, watching the lieutenant carefully dust and fold his handkerchief and put it back into his pocket, the crosshairs inevitably came to rest on the Russian's right breast pocket. The situation was conjuring an almost spiritual awareness of morbidity within him. The imminent act of killing seemed to stylize itself into a ritual, a poetry of the arbitrary transience of existence, as if when raised to an art form in the Japanese samurai code of Bushido.

With a strange lightness he reached the moment of decision, took the pressure point again, and with an inner smile squeezed the trigger.

As the bang rent the morning silence the young officer stared with shocked disbelief at the hole in his chest, from which a small fountain of blood was spurting. While his soldiers dived this way and that yelling loudly, he sank to his knees without a sound, his already empty eyes rolling up towards the morning sky, and dropped lifelessly into the bushes. After two of his men had paid with their lives for trying to recover him the others stayed under cover and withdrew without having located Sepp's position. But he knew that his hiding place was no longer safe and disappeared into the undergrowth fast, like a ghost.

During his daily explorations and hunts ahead of the main fighting line Sepp saw the enemy's numbers steadily grow. His reports and those of other marksmen were important pieces in the mosaic of German reconnaissance that managed to localize the focus of the coming attack.

At 08:00 on the morning of 26 September 1943 hundreds of flashes illuminated the eastern horizon with a devilishly twitching light. A rumbling and howling approached the German positions, rising to an ear-splitting pitch as it came. Between one second and the next the very entrance of hell seemed to open between the Landsers. In an almost single explosion an artillery barrage rained down on them from hundreds of guns and multiple rocket launchers. The air buzzed with splinters and it became hard to breathe amid the eruptions of earth, gas and dust. Nerve-rending cries of the wounded and mutilated followed the first wave of explosions, as the riflemen pressed as deep into their trenches and foxholes as they could. Quick prayers were murmured or screamed, silent promises were made, soldiers seized by hysteria were held back by their comrades. Minutes became hours.

The earth was trembling from the shell hits and detonations. The air turned into a stuffy mixture of dirt, gas and metal dust, which nearly took the soldiers' breath away. Sepp felt helpless as a little child as he clawed into the earth of his hole. Compulsively he murmured the Lord's Prayer again and again, interrupted occasionally by pleas for divine protection. 'Shit, shit, why me? God, let me come out of this alive, help me, help me. Our Father which art in Heaven…' Suddenly a huge detonation close by deafened him and momentarily robbed him of his orientation. A surge of earth and a dark shape fell in his direction beyond the trench's edge. Instinctively Sepp pulled his head to his knees and squatted down even more. Then dully something smacked into the dirt beside him. Abruptly he drew back, filled with icy horror. It was the steaming remains of a comrade from a hole nearby: a torso with its limbs torn off, its breast, neck and face torn apart by splinters into a bloody, twitching mess. But its mouth, amazingly unhurt, suddenly started to moan gutturally and talk as if from another world. 'What's wrong with me? What happened? Why is it so dark suddenly? Why can't I feel my body?' The shredded stumps of its upper arms and thighs twitched helplessly. 'Help, help me, please,' it gurgled imploringly. Panic came over Sepp. Almost hysterically he pressed into the wall of the trench to avoid touching the mutilated body. Paralyzed and unable to move, he stared at the nightmarish scene. The dying man started to scream: 'I'm blind, aaargh, blind, aaargh! Where are my hands? Aaargh!' With that the torso began twitching and rolling in the dirt. Sepp thought he would go insane. Suddenly he was trembling all over. His thoughts were screaming: 'Oh God, let him die, damn, damn, let him die, why doesn't he die?' The wounded man's cries increased to a last unreal '*Aaaaaarghhhhh*' and broke off amid a convulsive spasm of the shredded, former body. His comrade was released.

Sepp stared at the body as if hypnotized for several minutes as he tried to calm down. He was unaware of events around him, as the shells from tanks and heavy mortars contributed to the hellish scene. But now the infantry attack was approaching. As suddenly as the fire had started, after half an hour – an eternity for the Landsers – it ended. Now the rising rattle of Russian tank tracks could be heard, mixed with the sound of advancing infantry. It took mere seconds for the riflemen to recover. Medics took care of the badly wounded, while the slightly wounded and unwounded Landsers hoisted their weapons above the edge of their trenches and returned the Russian fire. Sepp was almost delighted at this opportunity to release his tension. Wildly, without any regard for danger, he threw himself into the fight to divert the madness that was growing within him. It was like being liberated.

Again, the hour of the marksman had come. Shot after shot his bullets found their mark in the enemy lines with deadly accuracy. The battle surged wildly and the front line dissolved. The barrel of his gun got so hot that the rust protection of grease between the barrel and the stock was melting and running over his fingers. Around him missiles were exploding and pieces of shrapnel were whining through the air. Instinctively he kept changing position, quickly grabbing the ammunition of fallen Russians as he jumped from one position to another. He also had to be sure not to lose contact with his unit.

To the simple soldier the connection between this Russian offensive and the breakthrough on the lower Dnieper was unclear. To Sepp, the whole strategical situation was reduced to the level of a primeval struggle for survival. For eight days the battle raged, shifting constantly from defence to counterattack. Companies and regiments dwindled away and were not replaced. The first aid posts were operating day and night, a never-ending stream of medics dumping bucketfuls of human tissue and amputated limbs in the waste pits behind the operating tents. Hundreds of soldiers waiting for help lay moaning, screaming and dying as the medical men separated out the hopeless cases. Those that were lucky awaited their deaths in morphine-induced tranquility, but most died alone and in agony. Many badly wounded men with no hope of recovery were actually shot on the battlefield by their own comrades, if they were lucky, because otherwise they were in danger of being found by the enemy. Mistreatment of the wounded was another feature of war's daily routine.

A smell of gunpowder, sweat, blood, fear and death lay over the battlefield and ate indelibly into the minds of the soldiers. Sepp, a 19-year-old youth, lost his innocence and his light-hearted view of life in these surroundings, like many others of his age. He accepted that he had to sell his life as dearly as possible, and he developed an amazing professionalism for one so young. He kept his nerve where other people panicked. He used his weapon with deadly precision, like a surgical instrument. A primitive instinct for battle surfaced within him so that the rhythm of defence, shelter and attack came as second nature. He was known for the fearlessness of injury or death that is also called bravery. And he had an unfathomable and essential share of luck. This is one of the mysteries of war: some soldiers seem to be immune from death or harm. Sepp was one of them. He would survive, despite the fact that he was always in the thick of the things.

On 4–5 October the fighting finally abated, allowing the exhausted company a few precious days to reorganize.

Chapter 4

The special gift of self-control

On 9 October 1943 the Red Army fell on the remnants of 3 Gebirgsjäger Division with twenty-fold superiority. The obligatory opening barrage – from 400 Russian artillery pieces and 220 multiple rocket launchers, firing more than 15,000 shells per hour – began at 10:00, subjecting the division to the nerve-racking horror of helplessness. Ghostlike, the riflemen emerged from the sulphur-steaming, churned-up earth as the bombardment ended, to defend their positions with desperate courage. Now it could be seen that true soldiers were the product of self-control, experience in battle, toughness, and the determination to see things through.

Like a tidal wave the attack stormed towards them. The Russian reservoir of manpower seemed almost inexhaustible. While the Wehrmacht's units withered away through lack of replacements, the enemy's fighting strength increased endlessly. Japan's decision to concentrate its attention on the southern Pacific meant that the Soviets could withdraw many troops from Siberia and deploy them in their western theatre. In addition they recruited every man aged between 14 and 60 without any exemptions. But many of the Russian units were created very quickly and were regarded as little better than cannon fodder. They were put into uniform jackets with their civilian clothes underneath them, and received just two days' training in the use of small arms. Their recruitment and organization was so rushed that not all of them even had weapons. Calculating the losses expected during an attack, only the first waves were given guns. The soldiers coming behind them had to set out unarmed and pick up the weapons of the fallen. The fear of being sent into action among those soldiers expected to fall was outweighed by an even greater fear of punishment, the Russians being mercilessly driven into battle by the secret services troops of the NKVD, who were posted behind them.

This battle was the first in which Sepp saw the Russians shoot their own deserters or, indeed, anyone who turned back, and how they drove the others forward into the defenders' field of fire without pity. One wave of attackers after another surged up against the German positions, to be shot down like rabbits. Subjected to this concentrated fire, the Russian dead and wounded began piling up in front of the German positions like walls. The ensuing waves of attackers then had to climb over their fallen comrades, using their bodies as cover, until the dead were piled so high that the attack actually began to falter as it came up against this ghoulish obstacle.

Tanks were sent in to get the attack moving again, driving through the barrier of piled bodies without any consideration for their own wounded soldiers. With a loud noise the bodies burst apart beneath the tracks of the T-34 tanks, their bones snapping like dry wood. The sight of the shredded bodies and the indescribable sound of moaning and screaming was unbearable. Rage grew within the combatants as the fight went on. The riflemen fought like madmen, just to avoid going insane at what they saw. When they ran out of ammunition they went for the enemy with bayonets and shovels instead. Such was the defenders' fury and determination that the Russians were finally forced to abandon their attack in the evening.

Being attached to the company commander meant that Sepp was always in the thick of the fighting. Often the distance between himself and the enemy dwindled so fast that he had to put down his sniper's gun after a few aimed shots and take up the MP40 which he always had slung ready on his back during such situations. Fighting of this sort was always very problematic for Sepp, because the front lines rapidly dissolved into close-quarter combat, and at distances below 30m the telescopic sight of his gun was virtually useless because its range of vision narrowed too quickly. Aiming below the telescopic sight through the open sight was not practicable either, because the telescopic sight restricted his range of vision to a very narrow slit. Consequently such situations placed a marksman under a disproportionate amount of stress, since he could not afford to lose his telescopic rifle and yet being seen with it exposed him to the special danger of being singled out by the enemy. Identified marksmen were invariably subjected to especially intense fire.

Towards evening the fighting died down, but the remaining riflemen could not relax because the Russians were obviously just regrouping ready for another attack. As it turned out they had only a few hours before the assault was resumed. This time it was more subdued, however, and the enemy was kept at a distance, the marksmen making an essential contribution with their well-placed distance shots.

During the night of 10–11 October the Russian fire abruptly broke off in the area around Sepp. After a few minutes a misleading silence fell. 7 Company's commander took the opportunity to make a quick tour of his men's positions in order to get an accurate idea of the situation. A machine-gun position that was placed slightly forward of the main line reported seeing suspicious movements in the bushes ahead. Immediately a patrol of eight experienced soldiers was sent out. Sepp, who accompanied them as a guard, crept along very carefully 30m to one side. He had his telescopic rifle with him, while the Landsers were equipped with machine-pistols and hand grenades. Their nerves tightened as they crept through the knee-deep grass towards the place the machine-gun team had described. After edging their way forward for about 300m they heard subdued voices. At a signal from the patrol leader Sepp took up a well-concealed position under a group of bushes, brought his gun into firing position and scanned the area through his telescopic sight. In front of him he saw the exit of a valley at a distance of about 80m. The patrol was heading for the ridge overlooking it. Carefully the patrol leader glanced into the valley and saw a group of about a hundred Russian soldiers, old men and teenagers, crowded together talking and smoking to conceal their fear and insecurity. They were led by an obviously inexperienced political officer. The patrol leader then crawled back and reported the situation to his men by means of signs. One of them crept up to Sepp, telling him that they wanted to try a surprise attack in the first light of dawn, despite their numerical inferiority. They expected that the Russians, being taken by surprise, would instinctively run to the valley exit, where Sepp could shoot them.

Two hours later the first pale light of morning appeared over the horizon. Many of the Russians were asleep by this time, their guards obviously inattentive. At a sign from the patrol leader every Landser took out three hand grenades and activated them. As if from nowhere, the twenty-four grenades exploded amidst the unsuspecting Russians. Immediately there was absolute panic. They ran in all directions, shooting wildly and hitting many of their own men. The wounded were crying out in horror. Then the patrol stood up and fired into the confused crowd with their machine guns. Just as had been expected, the Russians fled towards the valley exit and directly into Sepp's sights. Obeying the merciless laws of war, he did what he had to. His response was almost automatic: aim for the centre of the body and pull the trigger – aim and fire, quickly and repeatedly. Shot after shot found its target with deadly accuracy. Within moments five Russians lay in the grass, mortally wounded, while the others hesitated. Sepp reloaded, and another five went down. The rest pushed and shoved backwards, only to be cut down by the machine guns and grenades of the patrol. It went on like this for several minutes, until the massacre was at an end. Broken bodies and wounded, crying, dying men lay everywhere. Then, without a sound, Sepp and the patrol disappeared into the half-light of dawn like ghosts, without a scratch on them.

Their bold attack bought the decimated company a few hours of relief, but at midday the next Russian attack hit them with unabated violence. Once again they managed to hold out until evening with the courage of despair, until the attack suddenly stopped at the onset of darkness. Just before midnight they got news that the Russians had managed to break through the front at another point and were regrouping for a further deep thrust. For the riflemen this meant a temporary lull in the attacks on their own sector. But they had suffered considerable losses, and would not have survived another day of such onslaughts. Exhausted by hunger, wounds and disease, this respite was vital. For days they had lived on salted cucumbers and apples that they had found in Russian farmhouses. Even the most hardened constitutions were suffering from the effects of this unhealthy mixture. Everybody had diarrhoea. Because there was no chance of going to the toilet during the fighting, or of changing their underwear, every fart became a risk. Real dramas were played out in the trousers of some Landsers. With shitty pants, the circle of stinking comrades began to reorganize.

There was hardly a week in which to catch their breath, to get the necessary sleep, to see to some personal hygiene, and to recover their strength from fairly good food. The importance of personal hygiene in particular should not be underestimated.

The Wehrmacht had good reason to keep an eye on the physical condition of its soldiers. During training and when in barracks, its scrutiny included checks on the men's genitalia. The captain of the medical corps would make surprise visits with some ambulance men and the company had to gather in the canteen, where the soldiers had to undress and line up naked. The doctor would then examine their genitalia, looking for the first signs of venereal diseases, inflammation and mycoses that were the result of poor hygiene. Because a dirty penis meant disciplinary punishment, many were quickly spruced up with a handkerchief before attending the roll call!

Faced with the very real problem of keeping clean during periods of constant fighting it was vital for the men to see to their personal hygiene at every opportunity. Failure to do so could result in many unpleasant disorders, and more serious diseases could ensue. Mycoses, scabies, lice and boils all complicated the soldiers' existence. They took every opportunity to wash their clothes and remove the lice. The Landsers searching each other and their clothes for lice and other vermin became almost like a ritual. Two or three would sit together reverentially, a candle in their midst over which the lid of a shoe-polish tin was suspended from wire. The candle heated the metal lid like a hotplate. As the pests were found they were dropped on to the glowing lid to die with a loud hiss, to the delight of the gloating Landsers.

After a few days, in which the regiment had been able to only partially repair its defences, the riflemen were hit by the full force of a new Russian offensive and were once again subjected to a merciless fight for survival. Despite occasional German successes and counterattacks, the numerical superiority of the Russians soon began to tell, and terrain had to be given up at a steadily increasing rate. The destruction of the German positions was nevertheless very unsystematic, and there was a confusing ebb and flow of front lines until finally the point was reached where there was no longer any identifiable front line at all. Contact between the German units was severed. The outcome of battles became unclear and every unit seemed to be fighting on its own. It was a psychologically extraordinary, unstable situation, in which the enormous pressure of fighting while simultaneously fearing to be cut off brought with it the severe risk of panic. Uncontrolled flight would have resulted in catastrophe and annihilation, because then the enemy would have been able to push forward without meeting any serious resistance, and whole units would have been destroyed. The consequences would have been enormous losses in men and material.

At the same time panic is something deeply human, being the last instinct-driven attempt to save oneself from danger, albeit at the price of organized and cohesive resistance. For a military unit it meant the end. There is no possibility of preventing an outbreak of collective panic once it sets in. Once panic starts you need almost superhuman willpower to stand firm and control your desire to run away. And now, after two days of uninterrupted fighting, climaxing in the beating and stabbing of men with shovels and rifle-butts, the first signs of panic were appearing even amongst the Gebirgsjäger. Individual soldiers thought of running away, and some, succumbing to despair, gave up their will to live and were overpowered without putting up any defence.

Yet as the panic grew the officers and NCOs set an example by demonstrating their personal bravery and their will to fight. Only by leading from the front, standing side by side with their men, would they be able to prevent the disintegration of the unit. But this sort of leadership was part of the military ethos of 3 Gebirgsjäger Division, guaranteeing its survival as a cohesive formation until the very last day of the war.

Amid the carnage, Sepp watched in horrified fascination as two Russians leapt into a neighbouring trench where several of his comrades seemed to be paralyzed by dread. One of the Russians got his face split when one of the riflemen lashed out instinctively with a shovel, but the other proved himself an excellent bayonet fighter. With a catlike smoothness he parried every attack by the remaining six riflemen. Sepp tried in vain to help his comrades, looking in vain for the opportunity to get a clear shot into the confusing mêlée, but all he could do was watch as one after another they were stabbed to death. It was as if fate itself surrendered them to the Russian's skill and ruthless determination. Instead of co-ordinating their defence to stop him, they let him take them on individually. It was as if they had given up all hope of survival. It was not until the Russian had knocked down the very last rifleman and stood ready to kill him that Sepp managed to stop him with a well-placed shot. The surviving Landser looked up incredulously as the Russian's face burst, bone splinters and scraps of tissue splashing down on his face and uniform. Then, his will to survive having been restored by his unexpected rescue, the rifleman scrambled to join Sepp in his own foxhole.

This episode demonstrates one of the essential qualities required by a marksman. More than just the practical ability to shoot accurately he needed the special gift of self-control, to be able to act and react automatically even in situations that seemed hopeless. Though the ability to seek and take perfect single shots was essential, fast and precise handling of his weapon during a typical infantry fight was even more important. Because of this, good marksmen were more often experienced men than soldiers who were merely well trained in the technical and theoretical aspects of their role. Young marksmen who came directly from training and had no experience usually made about fifteen or twenty shots before they fell to enemy fire. The clumsy choice of a position that didn't allow for a rapid and concealed getaway, unwillingness to zigzag through enemy fire, and shooting from one position for too long were their most drastic mistakes. When a marksman was spotted his position was usually subjected to the fire of heavy infantry weapons such as mortars. If he could not withdraw without being seen, the only thing left for him was to run as fast as possible in the open. Among German marksmen this was called the *Hasensprung* ('rabbit jump'), because it involved jumping up suddenly and sprinting to the next position – which he should have picked out beforehand – in wild swerves and sudden unpredictable double-backs. This sprint through enemy fire demanded huge willpower and very strong nerves. Inexperienced soldiers usually stayed in their positions rather than risk it, and there they inevitably died.

Although 3 GD had fought well, the Red Army had achieved so deep a penetration to its south that it was in danger of encirclement. The Russians had driven a wedge deep into the German front and were now ready for the decisive stroke. At the last moment, just before the final assault began, the order to withdraw behind the Dnieper arrived on 31 October 1943. However, a bridgehead remained around the manganese mines near Nikopol to maintain the production of ore for as long as possible. This bridgehead was to be held by 3 GD and eight other divisions, all of them burned out and reduced to a quarter of their regulation strength. They had barely three weeks to prepare their positions and to organize the defence.

A few meagre supplies arrived, including among other things new winter uniforms. These were reversible cotton suits lined with cotton wool, one side being white for use in snowy conditions while the other was camouflage patterned for normal weather. But the soldiers' initial joy at receiving these warm clothes faded quickly. The thin cloth covering damaged very easily and the lining then soaked up moisture, so that the uniform not only became unpleasantly heavy but it also no longer kept them warm. When there was a frost the wet lining even froze. The same happened to the new felt boots. But soon they were faced with another problem: the padded material provided lice with nearly ideal conditions in which to escape the persecution of their human hosts. The suits became so full of lice that they and the lice got cleaned together at the beginning of spring. In addition they found that the suits could only be used in a 'dry' cold, or when they didn't have to move about too much. This was because they had to be worn over the soldiers' grey uniforms, so that they broke into a sweat after very little activity, and the sweat didn't dry out of the thick fabric easily. An increase of colds and influenza resulted. Unsurprisingly, when the division finally withdrew at the end of the cold season its line of march was marked by a trail of hundreds of discarded winter suits, and that was the end of padded suits for 3 Gebirgsjäger Division for the rest of the war. The Landsers found that they were better off with thick underwear, blankets, and tent squares.

In spring 1944 Sepp managed to persuade the regimental tailor to make him a camouflage shirt, which he used for a long time. He got a light snow-camouflage suit the same way, which he could roll very small and carry about easily. Its thin cotton cloth did not hinder his movements even when wet and it dried fast, just like the shirt.

Chapter 5

Never look death in the eyes unshaven

For a while fighting was restricted largely to patrols and the sniping of marksmen. To create anxiety in the Russian trenches Sepp went out hunting daily, making use of a knocked-out tank in the no-man's-land between the trenches. He would get under the tank before dawn, was protected by it during the day, and through a hole in the chassis he could observe and shoot at the Russian positions.

Unusually he had used his position under the tank for four days, scoring five hits in that time. Because the Soviets had no heavy weapons he felt absolutely safe in his position deep beneath the steel colossus, despite being conscious of the iron rule of marksmen against staying in the same place for very long. But the Russians had become extremely cautious by now and it had become harder for him to find a target. So on the fifth day Sepp decided to take an observer with him. He chose Balduin Moser, a Tyrolese, who had become his friend some weeks earlier. When they made their way to the tank position before sunrise they had no idea of the horror of the coming hours. Neither of them sensed the proximity of death that would seal the observer's fate that day. Sepp had, indeed, shot too many times from his supposedly safe position. The Soviets may not have had any artillery in the area to threaten Sepp, safe beneath his tank, but from now on he would face a far more dangerous adversary – a Russian marksman who knew his business as well as Sepp did.

Fiery red, the morning sun was blinking above the eastern horizon and sending its first rays across the deserted steppe as Sepp and Balduin settled down and began to scan the enemy's positions for a careless victim. It was just a tiny reflection of light from the lenses of Balduin's binoculars as they were raised a bit too high, but that was enough to tell the Russian marksman that the position was occupied. From his well-camouflaged position he brought his gun into a firing position and patiently awaited another flash of light. Less than a minute later he made his shot. It was a moment of realization on both sides, because at that very same moment Balduin, his binoculars to his eyes, whispered: 'Hey, Sepp, over there, two fingers to the side of the little mound, a mov...'. A second buzzing bang followed the first instantly, and there was a sound like a handclap next to Sepp. Blood and scraps of tissue splashed the left side of his face. He turned to Balduin and found himself looking into a demonic grimace. The Russian marksman's bullet had been deflected by Balduin's binoculars and had exploded directly in his mouth. It had torn away his lips, incisors, chin and half of his tongue. With panic-filled eyes he stared at Sepp, while a weird gurgle of foaming blood came from his shredded oral cavity. Seconds later another bullet exploded into the earth between them. Immediately Sepp scrambled back deep beneath the tank, pulling Balduin along by his feet. Leaving their position before nightfall was impossible, because it would have meant certain death at the hands of the enemy marksman. So they were doomed to wait. Sepp felt helpless, unable to do anything for his comrade's horrible wound. No bandage or pressure dressing would help here – his only hope was fast and professional help by trained medical personnel. But this was not within reach. Sepp could only watch as the remnant of Balduin's tongue swelled to the size of a child's ball, gradually blocking his respiratory tract. Sepp tried to press the swollen tissue to the side, but Balduin started to puke and got even less air. Only a tube or a cut in the windpipe could have saved him. So Sepp could do nothing but watch his comrade's futile struggle for life. It became steadily harder for the dying man to breathe and he sucked even more blood into his lungs with every convulsive gasp. Slowly he started to suffocate. Sepp tried to support his chest. Feeling helpless and useless he told him to hold out, and said that he would make it and that help was coming soon. As his death neared Balduin clung to Sepp's arm, his nails convulsively digging into his flesh, but Sepp did not feel it. It seemed like hours before Balduin finally looked at him one last time with an unfathomable depth and sadness, his eyes nearly popping out of his head. He clenched his hands in a strange manner in farewell, and a tremble ran through his body. Then his eyes glazed and his body went limp, freed from its torment. Frozen inside, Sepp stared down at the lifeless body he was holding. Minutes later the tension within him released itself in a crying fit as he unrestrainedly sobbed out his helplessness, his fear, and the constant strain of his daily fight for survival.

Paralyzed into inactivity, he spent the rest of the day next to his dead friend and comrade and kept vigil. His head was empty – no thoughts, no feelings any more; they were washed away by his tears. Finally he regained his composure and became a bit more pragmatic, harder and more merciless. At some point during this day that seemed to have no end he suddenly realized, looking down at his comrade, that he and Balduin had not shaved for several days. The face-wound surrounded by late adolescent beard stubble made the corpse look disgustingly ugly. It was the sort of intellectual absurdity that situations like these gave rise to. Sepp decided that he did not want to look that ugly as a corpse, if he should become one, and he swore that whenever it was possible he would shave daily from now on. He held on to this thought for the rest of the day as an emotional panacea. And he actually kept his word ever after – never look death in the eyes unshaven!

As dusk fell he pulled Balduin's body out and carried him back to camp under cover of the darkness. He reported in to the company commander and handed over Balduin's identity tag. In the morning he and another comrade dug a grave for Balduin. In the treeless steppe there was no wood for a cross, so they just put his steel helmet on the little mound. With Balduin, Sepp buried another part of his human innocence. Unconditional acceptance of the merciless laws of war was progressively growing within him.

The same night the tank wreck was wired for blasting by German engineers and the following morning it was ostentatiously blown up. This was done in order to deter the Russians from mounting an artillery strike against it themselves, which would have seriously endangered the German positions. This seems to have been the right decision, since the enemy remained quiet for a short time. But a few days later the next Russian offensive surged up against the riflemen's positions and over Balduin's grave. Tank tracks ground it into the earth and Balduin became one with the infinite Russian landscape and the anonymity of history, like tens of thousands of other soldiers whose young lives were torn from them.

The Russian attacks began on 20 November. They were mounted with less determination than before, so defence was no problem, but despite this they required the Germans' full attention and inflicted many casualties that further weakened their fighting strength. On the night of 24–25 November the Russians prepared for a far more serious attack that would embroil 3 Gebirgsjäger Division in yet another merciless vortex of iron and blood, especially in the area occupied by GJR 144. The Russians had gathered 200 tanks and several regiments of infantry in preparation, and fifty of the fighting vehicles would go for the area held by the 144th.

At 05:00 an artillery strike woke the riflemen from their light sleep. Instinctively they ducked into their holes. The barrage lasted about an hour, during which time each of them had to endure his fear alone. The Landsers clung to the earth, murmuring short prayers while the splinters buzzed around them. With the first light of dawn the shellfire ended abruptly and gave way to the rattling and squeaking of a large number of tank tracks. Equipped with hardly any weapons with which to fight tanks it took all the courage they could muster to hold their positions against two tank brigades and a mounted corps of Guards. The tanks rolled over the GJR 144's positions at the first attempt, the riflemen reserving most of their attention for the Russian infantry who were riding on their backs. Violent close-quarter combat erupted almost instantly once these tank-riders disembarked, quickly spreading as far as II Battalion's and 7 Company's respective headquarters. In their second wave the Soviets sent flame-throwing tanks. The infernal screams of the burned and wounded and the smell of scorched flesh undermined the morale of the surviving riflemen. Organized German resistance disintegrated, but every small group of soldiers fought on on its own, to the last bullet and the last knife. Hundreds of riflemen died under the cruellest of circumstances as the very last vestiges of ethical behaviour were cast aside. Nobody took prisoners and there was no consideration for the wounded.

While the character of the artillery fire had resembled the irresistible and inescapable power of Nature, facing the tank attack called for the last reserves of the Landsers' willpower and self-control. Every fibre of their bodies was tightened to breaking point, and an inner voice cried out to run away and escape as the dull ringing rattle of tank tracks increased in volume amid the silence following the artillery strike. The screeching sound of the tanks was soon joined by the dull explosion of shells. Adrenaline shot into the Landsers' veins and their muscles shook with anticipation as they methodically readied their weapons and grenades for the fight. The Russians were only a hundred metres away before the order came to open fire and the riflemen were able to release their tension. Already the tanks had rolled up. Sepp scanned the men around them and tried to identify the leaders by their equipment and weapons. Experienced Russian tank-riders would jump off immediately and take cover behind their tanks when fired on, which slowed down their attack, but if they stayed on board, overwhelmed by fear, Sepp kept shooting at them for as long as possible. He always finished with a shot into the spare petrol container that was attached to the tank's back. If the shot was a lucky one the petrol ran through the air vents into the engine compartment, which sometimes led to the engine self-igniting and brought the tank to a halt. Sepp and his comrades were shooting for their lives at whatever came in front of their gun barrels, but the Russian attackers came on regardless of losses. The riflemen had no weapons against tanks and their light mortars were useless against the assault. The enemy was getting rapidly closer and they could already distinguish the Russians' faces.

The defenders' concentrated fire kept the Russian infantry about a hundred metres away from their positions, but twenty tanks ploughed unstoppably on towards the riflemen in Sepp's area with an increasing rumble of their motors. The Landsers prepared the few hollow sticky charges they still possessed. Apart from these all they had were bundles of grenades tied together, which if placed under a tank's wheels could sometimes destroy the track and thus stop the tank. But all such defensive tactics required direct contact with the vehicle. To get that close required an extreme measure of self-control. Not until they were just 10m away were the Landsers' foxholes safe from a tank's weapons. Once it was within these last few metres the riflemen had to act immediately, because if the tank's crew made out where a foxhole was they tried to roll over it in order to cave it in and bury the occupants alive. Consequently the defenders' limited supply of anti-tank bombs were only given to the most experienced soldiers. When the critical distance was passed the riflemen went for the tanks, jumping up and trying to place their explosive charges on the turret, on the engine compartment, or amongst the wheels. But only few managed this, because the Russian infantry did everything they could to stop them. So only five tanks were disabled, grinding to a halt amid dully banging explosions. The others rolled on over the German lines. Anxiously, the riflemen shrank down into their trenches and holes.

Sepp crouched down in his own position as the iron colossi approached, squeaking and rattling. Not all of the riflemen managed to control their fears. Now and again one would jump up in the hope of escaping by wild flight, but the fire of the Russian infantry mowed them down without mercy. About 30m in front of Sepp a Landser leapt up to attempt such an escape but then wildly doubled back towards his comrades' trench. But halfway back a Russian machine gun cut him down. He tried to crawl on, propped up on his elbows, dragging his destroyed legs, while a T-34 rattled after him. Suddenly the wounded man stopped where he was, presumably to reserve his ebbing strength for a last desperate attempt to escape the tank. With his last vestiges of self-control he let the monster get within just a few metres and then rolled away to the side with all the strength and speed he could muster. Whether by chance or the intuition of the driver – a question without an answer, as is often the case in war – the tank managed to follow the wounded man's every move like a magnet, until he halted in pain and exhaustion. Then the tank's track caught his legs and drew them inescapably into its deadly embrace. With that the body of the Landser sat up as if he wanted to embrace his mechanical executioner. In seconds his limbs were gone under the monster. Horrified by the spectacle, it took Sepp a moment to realize that his comrade did not make a sound in his shock. When the track caught his pelvis the soldier showed his teeth like a horse, his face distorted into a diabolic, never-ending grin as his head swelled red like a melon. Then his body burst, uniform, bones and guts mixing to an ugly colour as his chest and head disappeared beneath the tank. What remained was no more than a hideous lump pressed into the ground, muddily churned up and amorphous, that would soon be sucked into the soil of Mother Russia, leaving no memory.

Then, to the defenders' amazement, the fighting vehicles continued on their way without taking any further part in the fight. Obviously there was a breakdown in communication between the tanks and the infantry, or they had temporarily misjudged the Germans' strength. Either way, with the disappearance of the tanks towards their rear the riflemen regained their courage and went for the unprotected Russian infantry with a vengeance.

Marksmen, being feared and hated, were badly mistreated if they were discovered. For this reason Sepp took precautions before every attack to ensure that he could hide his gun if he had to. On this occasion he had prepared a hiding place for it under some ammunition boxes. Just before the Russian attackers reached the German trenches he put his gun into the hole he'd prepared and unslung his MP40.

The Russians stormed into the riflemen's positions with roaring screams and a merciless close combat broke out. Driven by a primeval instinct of self-preservation the men fell upon each other. Rifle butts crashed dully into distorted faces, SMG salvoes turned stomachs into a bloody steaming mass, shovels ate into shoulders and backs, bayonets and knives were thrust into bodies. Amid screams, wheezing, moaning, gunshots, smoke, steam, sweat and the smell of blood, all humanity was lost, if it had ever been present in any recognizable form at all. Or was it the real face of humanity that was being revealed here? Man is after all just one of many vertebrates, just one part of the Darwinist struggle for survival governed by the simple rule of kill or be killed. Intelligence is just another weapon rather than a self-improving gift.

A dead Russian dropped into the trench like a sack of potatoes and bore Sepp to the ground beneath him. At the same instant another Russian leapt down, but the bayonet thrust that was meant for Sepp went into the dead man. Sepp rolled from under the corpse, the bayonet stuck in its ribs, as the Soviet struggled for a few seconds too long to yank his weapon free. Then Sepp was on him, kicking him in the genitals with the whole force of his pent up excitement. A dull crack, like the sound of a cookie breaking, told him that the metal toecap of his boot had broken his opponent's pubic bone. As the Russian fell on his back, doubled up in agony, Sepp grabbed his throat and crushed the larynx with his thumb, the Russian wheezing out his last breath as his eyes nearly popped from his head. From the corner of his eye Sepp saw a shadow heading towards him, and as he ducked instinctively the blow of a rifle butt ricocheted off his helmet. Momentarily dazed, Sepp rolled to the side and put his hands to his face as the Russian raised his rifle butt again, but the blow never came. Instead his attacker got a volley of sub-machine gun bullets in his back from very close by. Blood and scraps of tissue splashed all over Sepp. He jumped up just in time to see the comrade who had saved him getting a bayonet rammed through his kidneys and stiffening like a pillar of salt. In a raging, inexpressible fury, Sepp seized the gun of the dead Russian that lay before him and rammed the butt into the enemy soldier's face before he could pull the bayonet free.

In his rage Sepp lost all sensation of time and horror and even pain. At some point during the struggle a load of dirt had been blasted into his face as a hand grenade exploded nearby, and he felt a dull pain in his jaw and nose. Now, as the fight ended, he tasted blood in his mouth and realized there was a sticky mass of it all over his face and neck. The attack had ended as fast as it had begun. A handful of riflemen stood amidst a scene of bloody carnage that resembled a medieval battlefield, full of moaning, screaming, dying and dead soldiers. 'Sepp, old boy, you've come a cropper. Let me see.' A comrade examined his face. Sepp's right nostril was cut and in his lower lip were several tiny metal splinters. But there was no time to do anything about it right now. The next wave of Russians was already approaching with loud cries, so they grabbed the weapons and ammunition of fallen comrades and occupied a position 200m behind the front line, where they were joined by the survivors of other companies. Sepp had to leave his Russian marksman's rifle in its hiding place.

A small group of about twenty riflemen was less fortunate and was unable to reach them. Sepp saw them put up a bitter resistance until their ammunition failed, when the last five survivors emerged from their trench with raised hands. They were escorted away by the Russians with kicks and the blows of rifle butts.

Even though the situation looked hopeless, the riflemen had at least managed to separate the Russian infantry from their tanks. The latter were destroyed in a duel with German assault guns and an eighty-eight battery, so that threat to their rear was removed. By radio the surviving Landsers were told that two of the assault guns were now coming up in support, and when they arrived the regiment should mount an immediate counterstrike to retake their old positions. Both sides tried to regroup. Sepp was now armed only with a normal Mauser K98, but of course he was an extraordinarily talented and accurate shot, even without his telescopic sight, so he managed to hold off the probing attacks of single Russian patrols with rapid well-aimed shots that were camouflaged by the defending fire of his comrades.

Hardly an hour passed before the assault guns arrived and the counterattack was set in motion. Only about eighty riflemen remained fit enough to join the attack, supported by the two fighting vehicles, but the Russians had made a tactical miscalculation and had been unable to replace the casualties they had suffered in their own attack. They were visibly surprised by the sudden German offensive and fled back to their old positions, abandoning the captured trenches to the Germans. Sepp immediately went to look for his telescopic rifle and found it untouched beneath the ammunition boxes.

The German attack developed such momentum that their commander decided to push on against the Russians' positions. With his telescopic rifle back in his hands Sepp managed to gall the enemy with his fast and well-aimed fire, especially by picking out their leading personnel, so that they were unable to put up an effective defence. Without their tanks and heavy infantry weapons the Russian front line began to give way bit by bit as the Germans inflicted as many losses on them as possible. Many Soviets who thought themselves far enough away to be safe were hit by bullets from Sepp's rifle – what an irony of fate, since it was a Russian gun! In fighting situations like this camouflage was not relevant at all. The marksman would simply find a protected position with a good field of fire wherever he could, shoot for as long as possible, and then change to a new one as soon as he was taken under fire or the fighting line moved.

Only now, with the Russian attack thrown back, did a medical sergeant see to the wounds in Sepp's face. His nose was plugged and bandaged, and the metal splinters in his lip were pulled out with a magnet. But the wounds were not serious and Sepp stayed in the front line with his comrades.

The Russian line of defence dissolved in the face of the riflemen's determined attack, and Sepp forced his way into the enemy's positions with eleven comrades. They were no longer meeting any resistance and found only dead and badly wounded Russians. But the tension did not lessen, because the Russian positions contained well-protected dugouts in which enemy soldiers could be lurking in wait for them. Carefully covering each other, they approached one of these dugouts, from which strange gurgling sounds were coming. A rifleman shouted in Russian: '*Sdawajtesj! Wychoditje s podnjatymi rukami!*' ('Give up! Come out with raised hands!') When nothing happened he sprayed the dugout with fire from his MP40. Nothing was moving, but the strange sounds did not stop. Carefully the rifleman edged into the dugout, which was dimly lit through a hole in the roof. He had hardly put a foot inside before he called out to his comrades loudly. Entering,

Sepp was confronted by a scene of unbelievable cruelty. There were their five comrades who had been captured a few hours before. Foaming, gurgling blood was gushing from their throats, which had been cut a few minutes before so that their fleeing guards did not give themselves away by the sound of gunshots. Their arms and legs were twitching uncontrollably, their hands helplessly clawing at the earth. Sepp and his companions could not help them, and it seemed far too long before their suffering came to an end and their bodies went still.

It was events like this that made Sepp hard and merciless. They sowed the seeds of hatred within him that justified killing every enemy who came into the sights of his rifle, without exception. A feeling that was reciprocated on both sides. Everybody had motives of revenge with which to excuse their actions on the battlefield.

His comrades were not particularly compassionate either. Sepp observed how a captured Russian sergeant was subjected to the unbridled rage of Landsers who learned of the murder of the five prisoners. They wanted information about the enemy's positions, strength and plans. It didn't matter that the Russian didn't know about any of these things because of his lowly rank. It was really just an excuse to take revenge. Anyway, the information he gave was not good enough for the interrogating lieutenant and his assistants, and they beat his face to make him tell them more. Of course, he still didn't tell them what they wanted to hear, and even if he could have it wouldn't have been enough. They would just have found another excuse. The beatings became more brutal and the grilling degenerated into simple torture. Finally one of his interrogators came up with the idea of driving sharpened matchsticks under the prisoner's fingernails. His horrible cries of pain as they did so just encouraged the torturers even more. It was an experienced sergeant who put an end to it. Saying 'Stop that shit, you're no better than Ivan,' he pulled his 08 from its holster, put it to the Russian's neck, and pulled the trigger. The Russian's skull exploded, splashing his brains across their consciences. Even the lieutenant did not criticize this disregard of his rank. It was as if the sound of the shot released him from a trance.

On 27 November 1943 the Russians abandoned their offensive. The German bridgehead had been maintained, but at a considerable price. GJR 144 had been whittled down to a quarter of its theoretical strength. For nearly three weeks the bridgehead was left in deceptive peace. As winter set in the fighting diminished to occasional reconnaissance patrols, bouts of harassing fire, and petty skirmishes. But icy rain, mud, and finally frost and snow discouraged the exhausted Landsers.

Because they had no drinking water and had to drink from puddles and streams dysentery and jaundice became rife. What little drinking water they had was used carefully. Their morning toilet consisted of one mouthful of water from their water bottle. This they kept in the mouth. One bit they spat on their hands to wash them, a second bit they spat into the hollow of their hands to wash their face, and the rest was used to rinse their teeth and was then swallowed.

The men looked like ghosts. Sepp's once boyish face now resembled that of a 40-year-old. His eyes were sunk in their sockets, and his expression had become callous and bitter as a result of the inhumanity he witnessed daily. War had chiselled his features as if from granite. He was just 19 but he had the hardened face of a merciless veteran.

Now Sepp was hunting daily, his well-aimed shots inspiring fear and anxiety in the Russian lines. At the same time he was able to bring back important information about the enemy's tanks, artillery positions and troop movements.

While the Germans received few reinforcements or supplies, the Russians were able to bring up masses of men and material from the Russian heartland without pause or fear of hindrance. Thus they were able to mount a major new offensive against the German bridgehead on 19 December with ten complete divisions. Undisturbed by the Luftwaffe or anti-aircraft fire, Russian dive-bombers and fighters also participated in the attack. Never-ending waves of tanks and infantry surged up against the German positions, and in twelve days of endless fighting 3 Gebirgsjäger Division was almost annihilated. In places just two riflemen had to defend a hundred metres of front line against fifty times as many Russians. Added to this, the resistance of even the most experienced Landsers was being worn down by the strain of constant and uninterrupted fear. On 30 and 31 December there were several outbreaks of panic among the soldiers, but in this risky situation the regimental aide-de-camp and the Weaponry Officer proved themselves by their great bravery. They drove up to the front lines on a motorcycle and rallied the soldiers by their mere presence.

7 Company had been holding out against constant attack for days. Repeatedly changing his position, Sepp tried to force the Russians to

seek cover by fast shooting to ease the burden of his comrades. As if by a miracle he remained unhurt by the hail of enemy bullets, in contrast to his comrades. It was with horror that he saw how rapidly they were falling. Entire stretches of trench were now defended by just one or two men. In situations like this it needed very little to push a man into headlong flight. Dwindling supplies of ammunition, the sudden realization that one hadn't seen a single friendly face for hours, loss of contact with headquarters, the death of an officer, the lack of care for the wounded, the flight of comrades – all of these were enough to push a man over the edge. Sepp too felt the urge to seek supposed safety by flight, although he had the invaluable advantage of being able to move around freely within the area occupied by his unit. He could recognize his comrades' relief when he joined them for a short time. In their excited questions about the situation there were signs of suppressed panic.

At one point he was in a trench held by a single machine gunner, whose nerves were shot and who wanted to leave his position with Sepp when he went. 'Sepp, I'll go with you. I'm not mad enough to stay here and lose my arse. Shit, they don't get the wounded out, and we won't even talk about the lack of ammo and food.' At that moment they heard the put-put of a motorcycle behind them. Looking round they saw a captain lay down his motorcycle and run towards them in zigzags. Also at that same moment the nerves of the last five other soldiers in this part of the front broke, and they jumped up from their positions and ran towards the rear heedlessly. The officer recognized the seriousness of the situation instantly and, unslinging his MP40 from his back, he fired a volley over the soldiers' heads. The soldiers stopped abruptly and stared in shock at the officer. Suddenly one of them raised his carbine and fired at the officer, missing him. The captain, already having his MP in a firing position, took the Landser in his sights and said: 'Lower your weapons and get back to your positions, arseholes!' At that the Landsers came back to their senses, and lowering his own weapon the officer went over to the group. The sudden sound of a falling Russian mortar shell forced them to hit the dirt. Sepp saw the officer jump into the trench, and the soldiers followed him. Ten minutes later he crawled over to Sepp and the machine gunner. Filthy and exhausted, his presence nevertheless gave them confidence, even while a Russian salvo soared overhead and threw up fountains of earth behind them. Clods of mud pattered down all around. 'Men, don't do any shit, and hold out,' he said. 'We've got everything under control. The Ivans' pressure is decreasing. We've held out brilliantly so far. Now we're preparing a new defensive line in readiness for a tactical withdrawal. The lines of communication will be working again soon. Hold out as long as you can, boys. I'm relying on you.' He gave them a tin of chocolate and they pounced on it greedily while he disappeared in search of the next trench, dodging from cover to cover as he went. Half an hour later Sepp left the machine gunner in search of a new position. It was amazing what an effect the appearance of an officer had on the soldiers. The riflemen held out. A tactically disastrous and potentially deadly panic had been averted. The front line held.

But not all the soldiers held out under the constant strain. One way to escape the horror of the front was to fake a disease or a wound. There were men who specialized in this deception as if it was a science, and who shared their knowledge only with chosen comrades. For example, they learned that eating Nivea cream led to the same symptoms as yellow jaundice; and when deliberately wounding yourself by, for instance, a shot through the hand or the foot, they found that if you shot through a piece of *Kommissbrot* (army bread) it prevented the telltale signs of gunpowder burns round the edge of the wound. Ahead of major attacks or during constant fighting or adverse conditions the losses through faked injuries and diseases increased. Officers and sergeants were subjected to the same strains as their men and some routs were actually the result of soldiers being abandoned by their leaders.

Surprised by the Germans' steadfast resistance, the Russians broke off their attack on Sepp's sector and shifted their attention to the north-east to support a more promising offensive. But the German reconnaissance teams did a good job, so they knew about the transfer of the main area of attack. The few soldiers of the regiment who were still fit enough to fight were gathered from their trenches. It was with great satisfaction that they found the motorcycle-riding captain had told them the truth, and that a new defensive line really had been prepared.

The exhausted Landsers were laying around like sandbags in the relative safety of the assembly point when a medical sergeant came up. 'Men, now you'll get lead back in your pencils.' He went from man to man distributing small glass tubes containing pills, with a label that read 'Pervitin'. This is a methamphetamine, which suppresses feelings of hunger, increases stamina and dispels the need for sleep. 'Whenever you think you can't hold out any more,' he said, 'take one of those pills and your motor will start running again. But don't take too many, or else you'll flake out before you can say "peep". When you've taken one, then you'll be ready. So, have a good fight.' And with that he turned to see to some wounded men who were being brought in.

There were just a few hours left for rest and comatose sleep before they were pulled to their feet again and ordered to take one of the pills. With that they got a cup of hot coffee, their first for a long time, and there were even a few bottles of spirits going round, so that everybody got a good swig. But coffee and spirits always meant that bad news was about to follow. And so it was this time. Just half an hour later they were transferred to the sector threatened by the new Russian attack, where they were to support a harried infantry division.

Chapter 6

Mister Professor and his carbolic mouse

The thaw had started, and the riflemen had to make their way through a morass that was often knee-deep. Their shoes and trouser legs were so soaked with water and caked with mud that they could hardly move their legs. Physically exhausted, they dragged their feet along as best they could. Many of them were so tired that they slowed to a standstill and fell asleep where they stood. Their comrades grabbed them by the hand and pulled them on, and minutes later they awoke with a start and could not even remember how they had moved. The strain of the march was so overwhelming that even the pills, of which they were taking considerable quantities, had only minimal effect. Sepp carried his gun on his back, its telescopic sight wrapped with bits of a tent square to protect it from the mud, and around his neck was slung an MP40 in case there should be a surprise firefight. He had become accustomed to staving off his tiredness and hunger by chewing dry biscuits, which he obtained by swapping his cigarette ration when he could.

Behind the Russian moves there lay more than just a transfer of their focus of attack. Their operation developed into a huge offensive, which inflicted serious damage on the German lines on 30 January 1944. At the confluence of the Basawluk and Dnieper rivers two German armies were suddenly at risk of being encircled. As so often before, an urgent request to shorten the German front was refused by Army Headquarters for so long that when permission finally came it was almost too late. Fortunately the clumsy Russian leadership helped them by dividing the Soviet forces at the decisive moment instead of keeping them concentrated, and the German commanders were able to transfer sufficient units to the threatened sector to frustrate the attack.

The exhausted Gebirgsjäger plodded wearily on through the mud.

The higher purpose of their ordeal was not clear to them. Now they fought and marched without even thinking rather than because of any personal desire to survive. They had become warriors, bound together by comradeship and the ever-present threat of death.

There were no breaks any more. The riflemen were like zombies. In their wet winter fighting suits, their faces drawn by hunger and fatigue, they were just drawn along by the vortex of events surrounding them.

Sepp finally became sick. His constant exposure coupled with drinking water scooped from bomb craters gave him a severe bout of gastro-enteritis. Gripped by a shivering fit, he did not know from one minute to the next what he should do first, shit or puke. Captain Kloss, the battalion commander, found him shivering in the corner of his dugout, curled up like a wounded animal.

Captain Max Kloss had taken over II Battalion when it moved into the Nikopol bridgehead. Driven by a desire to serve the Fatherland wherever it was most necessary, he had volunteered to transfer from the Lapland Front to the Eastern Front. He was inspired by a firm belief that National Socialism was a good thing, and he wore a Hitlerjugend badge on his uniform as an expression of his conviction. But he was no blind party supporter, but rather a committed and brave soldier. When he saw Sepp squatted down and trembling, he asked the company commander who he was. The latter explained that Sepp was 7 Company's marksman, and that he was very good at his job. 'We need every specialist,' said Kloss. 'This man has to get fit again. He's the very last marksman we have in this mess. I can't lose him too.' Kloss told Sepp to go to the battalion command post and seek out the battalion runners. 'Tell the boys that they must care for you.' Then he turned to the company commander and said: 'I hope you don't mind, lieutenant.' The latter just shrugged. Still trembling, Sepp trudged away. It was only about a kilometre to the battalion command post, but he had to pause and shit again and again on the way. Finally he arrived at the runners' dugout, collapsed as he entered the improvised resting place, and moaned: 'The old man said you should care for me. In particular I need a new pair of underpants.' 'Of course, Miss Allerberger,' came a voice from the back of the cave-like room. 'Mister Professor and his carbolic mouse will come to powder your sore arsehole.' But they really cared for him. They got him black tea and found a highly effective diarrhoea medicine called Dolantin, produced by a company called Hoechst. This not only had a pain-relieving effect but was also antispasmodic. It considerably eased the painful side effects of diarrhoeic diseases. But Dolantin found its true destiny as a painkiller after the Hoechst chemists managed to increase its effectiveness by a factor of twenty at the beginning of the 1940s. This stronger version was given the name Polamidon. Germany's enormous need for pain-relieving medicine is witnessed by its production of 650 tons of the stuff in 1944.

Dolantin, rest and appropriate food eased Sepp's intestinal cramps and diarrhoea. The care he received from the runners was phenomenal, and in a few days he had recovered. Now and then Captain Kloss came round to ask about his state of health, and then they started talking and realized that they got on well with each other.

Sepp's legs were still a bit shaky, but Kloss said: 'It's time for you do something again. We've got four new sergeants. They're for your company. I thought you could take them under your wing, escort them over there and show them what to do. My driver will take you.' Less than a quarter of an hour later they set out in a VW jeep, but their ride ended after just a few minutes when a loud detonation rammed the steering wheel into the driver's hands with an iron fist. The car swerved to the left and tipped on to its side with a lurch. Sepp heard himself scream 'Shiiit!' as he and his comrades were thrown out into the mud at the side of the road. Everybody knew that they had driven on to a mine that had torn off the left front wheel, so nobody dared to move. They kept lying where they were. 'These fucking things must be ours!' said the driver. 'Yesterday it was clear through here, and Ivan hasn't got here yet. Anybody wounded?' Apart from some bruises they had all escaped unhurt. They crawled back to the car on all fours, feeling the ground carefully with their fingertips. They were discussing what to do next when a group of engineers came in their direction in single file. 'What are you housewives doing here?' said one. 'Did anybody say you could mess up our lovingly installed mines?' The brutal cynicism of this slender joke was not well received. 'You arseholes will get something in your face. You're supposed to tell us where you put our mines!' 'Well, now you know about them,' they were informed by the engineers' leader, 'and if you keep on grumbling we'll just leave you sitting there. I suggest you follow us very carefully.' 'Follow them,' said the driver. But the way to Sepp's company was now blocked, so the group returned to the battalion command post and reported to the old man. Thereafter Kloss kept Sepp at his personal disposal with the battalion runners.

The Russians did everything in their power to achieve their aim of driving the Germans back. Adherence to the rules of warfare disappeared along the Eastern Front and was replaced by inhuman brutality. The Soviets determined the new rules of engagement and set about paying us back for our early successes against them. In the process they demonstrated often inhuman harshness towards their enemy, not just against the soldiers but against the civilian population too.

Railwaymen had managed, despite heavy bombardment, to bring up two batteries of Gebirgs Artillerie Regiment 112 as urgent reinforcements to the bridgehead. But just one locomotive had come through the bombardment intact, and on its last trip it was to evacuate the seriously wounded from the pocket. Sepp and his comrades passed the railway depot on the way to their new positions in the early morning. Hundreds of wounded were thronging around the wagons, very inadequately cared for. When they saw the small unit of riflemen still fit to fight, a look of hope came into their eyes. One spoke their thoughts out loud: 'Hold Ivan back until the train is out!' Though the effect of his words on the Landsers was almost imperceptible they provided the necessary motivation they needed to hold out against the coming attack for as long as possible.

The Soviets were only a kilometre and a half from the depot, and the riflemen deployed from their line of march under fire and took up the fight. The train got away literally at the last minute, under direct bombardment, but only a few kilometres further along the track Russian fighter-bombers attacked the helpless train, dropping their deadly payloads without any regard for the red crosses it bore. The wagon carrying the medical personnel was hit first, the bomb killing almost all the doctors. Amid a hail of bullets and bombs the stricken wagon then pulled the rest of the train from the track. Its wagons crashed into each other and spat out their loads, leaving wounded men lying helplessly in the dirt. The next morning their own withdrawal led Sepp and his comrades past that place. Before them lay a scene that was uncommon even amid the daily horrors of war. Strangely contorted corpses hung from the wrecked train, torn off limbs lay all around, bandages were scattered everywhere, fluttering in the wind. In their panic the survivors had tried to drag themselves away, but most were not fit enough to endure the strain. Their wounds tore open again and they bled to death. Life trickled away. Their bodies lay scattered over the ground in a circle about 300m wide. The few surviving medical personnel, including just two doctors, were helpless in the face of such a disaster, but hope returned when they saw the riflemen coming. But there were just fifty of them – some of whom were also wounded and bandaged – and compared to the magnitude of the situation they represented a mere drop in the ocean. Added to that the Russians were after the little fighting group and would catch up with them in about an hour.

As fast as they could they improvised stretchers to carry the wounded. Cruel as it might have been for those concerned, they had no choice but to help only those fit enough to walk and those with the best chance of survival. All the wounded who were almost dead or who were unlikely to survive being moved had to be left behind. Twenty-four hours earlier the Landsers had envied the wounded in a way, because they were out of the fighting and theoretically on their way home. Now the war had caught up with them again, and had made them comrades in a renewed fight for their lives.

Suddenly a gunshot broke the silence. Everybody looked in the direction of the sound and saw a rifleman with an 08 in his hand standing petrified beside a now dead man. Sepp was already next to him, asking what he'd done for Heaven's sake. The Landser sank to his knees, sobbing unrestrainedly. He needed a minute to regain his composure before he could report. The dead man had been his friend and neighbour. Both his legs had been amputated, and the stumps had been bloodily torn open again by the crash. In addition his chest had been ripped up by splinters. It was incredible that he had survived these wounds for as long as he had. It was clear to him that he would be one of those left behind to the Russians' mercy, and when he saw his friend he asked for a last good turn – a fast release from his sufferings. He begged so urgently that the rifleman did him the favour, though he knew it would haunt his memory for the rest of his life.

The rest of the company was now ready for the march and they left this place of misery, hoping that the Russians would care for the wounded or at least shoot them quickly.

Sepp got out his telescopic rifle and dropped back a bit to cover the group's rear. They'd been walking for about half an hour when Sepp, following about 500m behind, hid in a bush to look around. That was when he saw a Russian patrol at a distance of about 150m. He had to act fast to force them to stop. He took careful aim with his rifle resting in the fork of a branch. He had a difficult field of fire, interspersed with bushes that the Russians were cleverly using as cover. Practice, intuition and the feeling of an experienced rifleman for the right moment really paid in situations like these. Quietly, he aimed at the patrol leader with his telescopic sight, the reticle resting on his breast and following him through the bushes. There it was, the right moment. The Russian had stood in the open for several seconds, and Sepp's shot hit him in the chest and threw him backwards into the bushes. The others were experienced enough to immediately recognize the work of a marksman. They scattered like chickens attacked by a hawk and hid themselves as well as they could. Quickly Sepp put shots as near as possible to two more whose position he could make out, hitting the water bottle that one had hanging on his belt. That was enough to pin them to the ground for half an hour. Then Sepp quickly rejoined his group and reported that the enemy were near. A small detachment immediately joined him at the rear, but amazingly they were not bothered again.

As dusk gathered they met another battalion of riflemen that had also left the enemy behind, and together they were ordered via radio to take position and stop the pursuing Russians for as long as possible.

Chapter 7

Just another pre-planned catastrophe

In this other battalion Sepp met a colleague he already knew of by hearsay. This was the marksman Josef Roth, a Nürnberg man of his own age who had volunteered to join the Gebirgsjäger and, like Sepp, had come up with the idea of becoming a marksman after capturing a sniper's rifle. The two immediately got on well with each other. Roth's battalion commander knew the value of correctly deployed marksmen in a defensive position and he gave them a free hand. While the rest of the troop entrenched they agreed on a joint reconnaissance of the enemy's movements and to work together in the coming battle. It turned out that two pairs of trained eyes saw much more than one.

At about 08:00 the next day a shot suddenly whizzed among the riflemen as they were busy strengthening their positions and a lance corporal collapsed to the ground with a scream, twitching. Fast as lightning the others threw themselves into cover. Only one Landser stayed with the wounded man for a fatal few seconds too long. He didn't hear the bang of the bullet that went into his skull behind the left eye and came out of his right eye, leaving a hole as big as a fist. A yellowish mass of blood and brain surged from it as he fell. There was a warning cry of 'Look out, sniper!' Helplessly the lookout guards let loose a hail of machine-gun fire in the supposed direction of the sniper, but without effect – as was proved by the well-placed headshot that brought down one of the gunners moments later. Nobody dared to move. Sepp and Josef were still in their dugout when a runner rushed in and breathlessly reported the sniper attack. The battalion commander just said: 'Riflemen, you know your job. Solve the problem!' Moving quickly, and making careful use of cover, the two hurried to the front line with the runner.

He led them to a section of trench that was already finished, where they were welcomed by a sergeant who gave them a report of the events of the past few minutes. A little to one side a piece of sap ended in a well-camouflaged observation position in a thicket. Sepp and Josef were able to reach this post without showing themselves, and they started to scan the area for signs of a possible marksman's hiding place. Despite straining their eyes they saw nothing suspicious, even though they paid special attention to one particular area because of where the first of their comrades had been hit. Still nothing. Hours passed. They discussed where they would position themselves if they were the Russian marksman, but even the seemingly ideal location they would have chosen showed no signs of movement.

At around noon another rifleman was hit while throwing his tin of shit over the edge of a trench, but this time the victim was lucky, the projectile glancing off his helmet to strike his upper arm. Luckily the Russian marksman hadn't used an explosive bullet, as was more usual, so the Landser escaped with a gaping flesh wound.

Josef and Sepp had been looking through their binoculars towards the Russian lines at the time and both saw a patch of grass sway as the pressure wave of the Russian marksman's shot disturbed it. They admired their opponent's imagination: he had clearly hidden himself in an earth cave dug through a dam. But now the question was, was he experienced enough to leave his position or would he stay there? The latter possibility seemed to be indicated by the fact that all of his shots had clearly been made from the same direction. So Sepp and Josef decided to lure him into showing himself. They settled on providing him with a fake target that would be exposed by a comrade. Josef would take position about 50m away from Sepp, and they would both shoot into the enemy's supposed position as soon as the grass moved when he fired. They stuffed a bread bag with grass and put it on a stick, on top of which they placed a cap. Josef handed the dummy to a comrade and told him to hold it carefully above the trench's edge in exactly ten minutes. Both marksmen then readied themselves and were aiming at the assumed position of their enemy when the cap appeared above the trench's edge exactly on cue. And their cunning paid off. The Russian shot too early, not calculating on a trap, and from the same position. He had hardly fired when both Sepp and Josef shot at nearly the same moment. They had each loaded their Russian marksmen's rifles with one of the few captured explosive bullets they had. Away in the earth cave there was a dull thud.

Attentively they watched the small earth dam through their telescopic sights and saw hectic activity behind it as something was carried away. A curious Soviet observer appeared with binoculars on his eyes and immediately paid with his life. Bullets from the two German marksmen's rifles simultaneously hit his head, which burst like an overripe pumpkin under the force of the double impact. Only his binoculars remained, lying intact on the edge of the trench. Now it was the Russians who did not dare leave cover, and the Landsers were able to finish their trenches without further interruption.

Sepp and Josef prepared well-camouflaged alternative positions for the coming Soviet attack, dividing the approaches so that they could give each other covering fire. In order to remain unseen for as long as possible they agreed to maintain a crossfire until the enemy was about 100m away, and then to switch to straight approach fire. This strategy worked well and contributed to the troop holding out for two days, which enabled the evacuation of their own wounded and those they had rescued from the train. But bit by bit the bridgehead around Nikopol gave way and once again encirclement threatened. As their respective units were now regrouping Allerberger and Roth had to split up. Knowing the special hardship and strain that faced marksmen, they shook hands for a very long time and wished each other the essential luck they required to survive the war. Then they parted, hoping to see each other again one day.

But they had learnt an important lesson from their encounter: there are situations in which co-operation with a second man, a special observer, is a huge advantage. Although Sepp had sworn to only work alone after Balduin Moser's death, he had to admit that teamwork was advantageous. Sepp therefore convinced his company commander of the value of having an observer with him, and thereafter whenever he needed an observer he was allowed to choose one from among his experienced comrades.

As the hard fighting continued, GJR 144 again and again had to lead diversionary attacks to keep important traffic junctions free for withdrawing units. Though it was bled white in these operations, it was a testimony to the regiment that it was able to hold its assigned positions against the massive Russian attacks. Sometimes the Landsers even succeeded in mounting small counterattacks. But the weakened regiment suffered enormous losses, so that its very existence was endangered. Entire companies were destroyed to the last man.

After four days of severe fighting, on 12 February 1944 they got the order for a general withdrawal from the bridgehead. The regiment was so decimated and had been without supplies for so long that it had no heavy weapons left and every Landser had only about five or ten cartridges for his personal firearm. Under such circumstances, when it was harassed by the enemy its few marksmen became the unit's 'artillery'. Only they were able to form a rearguard that could hold the enemy at a respectful distance. In order for the marksmen to keep fighting every Landser gathered up Russian ammunition wherever he could.

Only with great effort and huge losses did 3 Gebirgsjäger Division escape from the pocket and reach the new front line on the Inhulets. The weather changed and became an enemy and an ally at the same time. It was an enemy because a storm of snow and ice began that threatened to annihilate the physically exhausted riflemen, who had to face it without any protection following their withdrawal. But it was an ally because any attempt at organized pursuit became impossible under such circumstances.

Apathetically the Landsers staggered across the steppe, the ice crystals stabbing into their faces like needles. The thermometer sank to minus 50°C. Anyone who stopped moving or fell to the ground with exhaustion had frostbite within a few minutes, which often proved lethal. The iron fittings of their mountain boots transmitted the cold right through to their feet. Boots, sweaty socks and skin froze together. Many of those afflicted thus could only move by crawling. The medics were unable to help them much, because all their liquid medicines had frozen in their containers. Only for the worst cases did they have a few morphine ampoules that they carried in their mouths to keep them warm. Wounds immediately froze and became icy. There were fights over the winter clothing of Russian corpses found frozen in the snow, and lucky was he who could get a felt cap or felt boots this way.

Uncompromisingly the riflemen kept each other moving. As soon as Sepp paused he was kicked by a boot or hit with a rifle butt and he likewise hit anybody who tried to stop. Despite these measures many soldiers got frostbite or even died, so weak had they become. The number of those fit to fight dwindled daily. With great effort the wounded were dragged along for as long as they had any chance of recovery. Those who would die anyway were mercilessly left behind, as all the baggage animals had been eaten. Their weapons, covered with ice, were useless. The extreme cold made the steel shrink so that they could not even move the bolts. The high quality of the German weapons, with their well-engineered, close-fitting parts, worked against them now. The Russian weapons by contrast were constructed with greater tolerances, and worked even at temperatures below zero. The stone-hard frozen ground even prevented the preparation of defensive positions. Only animal instincts of self-preservation drove the riflemen on through the depressing steppe, while the storm constantly increased. As if in a trance, numbed by hunger and exhaustion, Sepp stumbled on through the knee-deep snow, his hood pulled down round his face, his padded camouflage jacket pulled close about him, and his marksman's gun on his back wrapped in a cover. The cold was almost unbearable.

Ahead, the shadowy silhouettes of a farm and a huge pile of straw emerged from the grey haze of the falling snow, and at that moment the ground below him suddenly gave way. With a cry he fell into a hole that had been covered with snow and found himself staring into the frozen face of a dead Red Army soldier, distorted to an ugly grin. He scrambled back to the surface again like a beetle, digging his way out from the snow on all fours. Now there was also movement in the burned-out farm that was only 30m away. As if electrified, the riflemen jumped to protect themselves, but their frozen hands could not get hold of their weapons, which were ice-covered and unusable anyway. The rag covering Sepp's rifle had proved itself useless. Scraps of Russian conversation were carried to them by the wind. Everyone stopped, anxiously waiting for the Russians to open fire, but nothing happened. Minutes of terrifying uncertainty passed, until it became obvious that the Russians were not in a fit state to fight either. Both parties withdrew carefully.

Night was falling and the snow was coming down even more heavily. Protection from the weather became their prime consideration. Instinctively the Landsers approached the huge pile of straw, their only potential protection from the roaring force of Nature. Then came the point when they threw all caution to the growing wind: they had to take shelter from the storm. A few more steps and they were there. Quickly they burrowed into the warm straw and huddled together there like young pigs, and so survived the storm. For two days and two nights it roared on unrestrained and even the rules of war had to bend to its will. The pile of straw became the refuge for the Russians, too, who crawled into its shelter from the other side. Unable to fight, the Landsers and their remorseless foes were separated by no more than a few metres of straw.

On the morning of 20 February the storm abated and they found that their weapons, protected from the cold, now worked again. Nervousness spread among the Landsers at the thought of their impending fight with the Russians on the other side of the pile of straw, because nobody knew how and when it would start. Three riflemen dug their way out to make a reconnaissance. When they returned half an hour later they gave the all clear, obviously relieved. The Soviets had withdrawn in the early morning.

Again they trudged on through the snow to their new fighting area. The physical condition of the Landsers declined at an alarming rate, but at the last minute the regiment reached a supply depot and obtained ammunition, food, clothes and blankets. They even got small numbers of replacement personnel. They settled down in the ruins of a village for several days.

Since he belonged to the battalion staff, Sepp benefited from access to such luxuries as a strong dugout and even an oven. He was daydreaming in a cosy corner when Captain Kloss returned from a regimental meeting. Shivering with the cold, he sat down in front of the oven and stretched his feet in their wet boots closer to the warmth. Then tiredness overcame him and, leaning back against the wall, he fell asleep. Some time later Sepp looked over and saw that Kloss's boots were smoking. Then the officer jumped up with a scream and leapt around shouting: 'Shit, shit, that's hot!' He tried to take his boots off but failed, because the wet leather had dried too fast and had shrunk around his feet. The only thing left was to pour a bucket of water over them so that the leather could expand again. The soldiers present grinned broadly at this solution to the crisis. Fortunately clothing replacements were among the supplies that had been received, so Kloss was able to change from his leather boots into some new felt ones.

On 25 February the Russians attacked again, but the attack was halted by a successful barrage from the now operational mountain artillery regiment. The riflemen used the ensuing lull to withdraw back to the new front line on the Inhulets. As had happened so often before, several decisive mistakes had been made when laying down this new front line. While the front line officers were able to develop practical strategic and tactical concepts by correctly analyzing the situation and estimating their resources and the enemy's strength, the Army High Command staff at OKH (*Oberkommando des Heeres*) again and again torpedoed their solutions by issuing ludicrous orders to hold unnecessary positions. The consequences of these irresponsible decisions were huge losses of material and human lives that could not be replaced. The army's overstrained logistics could not compensate for losses on such a scale. Military operations were compromised and dwindled into an uncoordinated withdrawal that became more and more chaotic and ended with everybody saving himself in any way he could. The new front along the Inhulets became just another pre-planned catastrophe. Shortening of the line in order to preserve it was prohibited, essential reorganization of their forces was not carried out. So the Russian attacks were awaited by an overstretched and thinly defended front line. Units with a high fighting morale and considerable experience, such as 3 Gebirgsjäger Division, became the great white hope of commanders in these situations. Consequently they were thrown into the heart of the battle again and again. The entire responsibility for stopping the enemy breaking through and preventing encirclement rested on their shoulders. Back-up positions and reserves could only be improvised and provided no real operational security. The price in personnel and material was immense.

On 1 March the Soviet attack crashed into the riflemen's positions again. The Russians' determination seemed to be especially intense this time. In the area held by 3 GD and the neighbouring 16 Panzer Grenadier Division the Soviets were able to constantly replace their losses. Up to a thousand new soldiers were added each day, while the German losses could not be compensated for. On the third day of the attack the armoured division's infantry were virtually destroyed by the Russians and the Gebirgsjäger riflemen had to defend their area too. By the fourth day the division had been reduced to half its fighting strength. By a miracle Sepp remained unhurt apart from cuts and bruises, although he was always at the centre of the action. Once again it was proved that high morale and experience could compensate for material superiority for a long time, but by the end of the fifth day Sepp's battalion had dwindled to just sixty fighting men.

While they fought on against the enemy, who was attacking them from two sides, the sound of fierce fighting suddenly arose to their rear. At the same time a signaller received a radio message in which the battalion headquarters reported a Russian attack and called for help. It seemed that an enemy combat group had managed to infiltrate the riflemen's front and was now trying to neutralize the control centre of the German resistance. Outnumbering them by one hundred to thirty, the Soviets totally surprised the headquarters detachment, which was not prepared for such an attack. A violent firefight developed, in which the ammunition of the defenders was quickly exhausted, and more and more men fell to the raging fire of their assailants. The attack on the main fighting line was by then ebbing to a long-range firefight, so that the company commander risked sending a few men to support the defenders of the command post. He also contacted the neighbouring companies, which sent a few more men. Quickly a small force of just twenty riflemen was assembled, among them Sepp and a comrade experienced in combat patrols, who would support him as an observer.

It was now about 07:00, and it was decided to mount the counterattack at 08:00. A short hour later the riflemen moved off as fast as possible, but with all necessary care, in the direction of the command post, which was less than a kilometre and a half away. After fifteen minutes they encountered the Russian combat group.

In a bushy, slightly hilly area the command post lay in a valley at the foot of a steeply rising hill. This could not be occupied by the inadequate German units, but for the Russians it held a high strategic value, because from its top they would be able to control the German positions. The defenders had withdrawn to a last fortified dugout and were down to their last few rounds. Now they replied to the furious fire of their attackers with just single aimed shots. The approaches to the base were covered with corpses from both sides.

The Gebirgsjäger relief force paused to get an overview of the situation. Now was the time for the marksman and his observer to prove themselves. Sepp and his comrade quickly chose a group of bushes that provided them with good camouflage but had a clear view of the battlefield. The plan was for the riflemen to commence their attack while the two of them eliminated as many of the enemy as possible. The observer had a very wide range of vision compared to the very limited one the marksman had through the lens of his telescopic sight. With his better overview of the scene the observer could clearly increase the effectiveness of the marksman by giving him exact aiming instructions. Sepp had barely raised his weapon into a firing position when he saw a Landser he had supposed to be dead from a bloody head wound trying to raise himself on his hands, only to be immediately hit by a Russian machine-gun salvo. His head and neck turned into a bloody mass under the impact of the projectiles. Sepp's observer had already identified the gunman: 'Small earthwork, 10m right.' Sepp swivelled his gun and took the Russian into his sights, the reticle coming to rest on the Russian's partly exposed chest. His shot hit its mark at 150m with fatal certainty.

His shot was the signal for the relief force to attack. The riflemen opened fire, while Sepp's bullets hit every enemy his observer could find. The ensuing fight was short but violent. Suddenly the Russians lost sight of their goal amid the unexpected crossfire and mounting losses, and, shooting wildly in all directions, they withdrew after a few minutes. About twenty of them were seen to disappear into the trees. They left eighty dead and wounded behind. The riflemen had no time to do any more, and after a short consultation with the survivors of the headquarters troop they headed off. Twenty minutes later they were back with their comrades in the main fighting line.

For six days the fight had surged against them almost without pause and the Landsers were exhausted, so that they fell into a deep, coma-like sleep as soon as they were inactive for even a few moments. Often in situations like these the medics distributed the stimulant Pervitin to mobilize the riflemen's last physical reserves.

3 GD managed to hold its positions until 7 March, but already on the 6th the Soviets had crossed the Inhulets in neighbouring sectors and had burst through the German front line. Now the riflemen were sticking into the Russian line like a thorn that had to be pulled out quickly. With more and fresh infantry forces the Russians stormed the German positions. The mountain riflemen of GJR 144 were pressed back until they stood in furious close combat that extended even to the regiment's headquarters. Coherent command became impossible. Every group fought on its own and for plain survival. In the midst of this confusion the order arrived to withdraw across the Inhulets immediately.

In the meantime the Russians had managed to cut 3 GD's line of retreat almost completely. Their supplies were destroyed and the division's main first-aid post was overrun. There remained a single defended corridor about half a kilometre wide through which they could withdraw. The few survivors of the 144th still fit enough to move commenced a fighting withdrawal. Scattered soldiers and men from other units joined them as they went.

Among them was a group of four medics who had escaped the Russian attack on the divisional first-aid post. These men were clearly totally worn out, and demonstrated obviously disturbed behaviour, the product of the psychologically distressing experiences they had endured. A sergeant who wanted information about where they had come from and what had happened got only jumbled sentences in reply and he handed them over to other medical personnel as soon as he could. 'Medics, care for your mates. I think they've seen the Holy Ghost, the way they're talking. They need a drink and a hit in the neck, but try to do it with motherly kindness. Perhaps they'll tell you what happened.' And in fact some food and alcohol calmed them down. But their description of the events they had witnessed frightened their audience and increased their fears of possible Russian imprisonment.

It seemed that far from all the German wounded had found a place in the last train that tried to escape from the Nikopol pocket. In particular the hopeless cases had been left at the main aid station with a doctor and seven ambulance men. To indicate their defencelessness they had put up a white flag and the flag of the Red Cross and piled their weapons in a clearly visible heap in front of a tent. It was a Mongolian unit that came up and occupied the place. Carefully running from cover to cover, they had surrounded the aid station and demanded that the Landsers came out with raised hands. '*Wychodite s pidnjatymi rukami, faschistskie swinji.*' ('Come out with raised hands, you Fascist pigs.') Two ambulance men stepped in front of the operation tent. From a Russian language book issued to soldiers on the Eastern Front they had picked out some phrases that they shouted over to the Soviets: '*My ne wooruscheny. Sdes tolko ranenye. My sdajomsja Sowetskoj Armii.*' ('We unarmed, here only wounded, we surrender to the Soviet army.') Screaming something unintelligible at the Landsers, the Mongolians approached with their weapons in a firing position. Hands above their heads, the two ambulance men awaited them, their knees trembling obviously. The first Mongolian reached them and screamed an order that the medics could not understand. Mere seconds passed, and then he hit one of them in the face with his rifle butt without warning. Moaning, the soldier fell down, blood from his broken nose and split lips streaming between his fingers as he pressed them to his face. The Russian kept screaming and kicked the man lying on the ground. Obviously his reaction was not what was required of him, because suddenly the Mongolian stepped back, aimed at the soldier with his machine pistol, and shot him in the chest. The medic collapsed, his life seeping away with a bloody wheeze. At this moment the doctor, in a bloody apron, and another ambulance man stepped out of the tent to see what was happening. This distracted the shooter, while four other Soviets came up and pushed the Germans back into the tent screaming incomprehensible orders and pushing the barrels of their guns into their backs.

On the operating table lay a wounded man with serious head wounds who was being tended to by another medic following his operation. One of the Mongolians pushed him away, pulled a knife from his boot, and thrust it into the wounded man's chest, saying: '*Eta faschistskaja swinja bolsche nam ne pomecha.*' ('This Fascist pig won't bother us any longer.') He rammed his knife into the man's heart two or three times before withdrawing it. The Germans looked on in shock, with a dreadful premonition of what was about to ensue. They were pushed into the neighbouring tent, in which the wounded were lying. A Mongolian sergeant pushed the doctor aside as he tried to persuade them to spare the wounded, and shouted: '*Seijtschas my wam pokaschem, kak postupajut s ludmi, kotorye napadajut na matuschku-rossiju i ubiwajut schenschtschin i detej.*' ('Now we will show you what happens to those who have attacked Mother Russia and killed women and children.') Signalling to his soldiers with a wave of his hand and indicating the wounded, he commanded: '*Perereschte im glotki, kak owzam.*' ('Cut their throats like sheep.') It sent shivers down the Landsers' spines when they saw the demonic gleam in the eyes of the two approaching Mongolians. They must have been experienced shepherds and butchers, because they took knives from their boots that they had obviously brought from home, and they knew how to use them. They were the ideal tools for the following apocalyptic deed. Without the slightest sign of emotion they went over to the wounded and with well-honed expertise yanked back their heads and cut deeply into their throats of their helpless victims. The sharp knives sliced into the flesh with such ease that in some throats the bones of the spine could be seen through the gushing blood. The Mongolians worked fast and methodically and after a few minutes the whole tent had been transformed into a slaughterhouse. The dying Landsers writhed with pain on their beds. The doctor, though he was confronted by the gruesome horrors of war every day, changed colour to a greenish-yellow shade and could not stand any longer. '*Smotri*,' ('Weakling') shouted the sergeant, and beat his gun butt into the kneeling man's face. Like a match the doctor's nosebone cracked and blood shot from his face, splashing onto the sergeant's boots. '*Na moi sapogi, slaboumok, ty, staraja swinja!*' ('Swine, look at my boots!') With that he grabbed his machine gun by the barrel and brought the butt down on to the doctor's head. A crack like a split in an overripe melon revealed a break in his skull. Two or three more well-aimed blows with the metal butt and the doctor was dead. Frozen with horror, the ambulance men stood in the corner. One was pulled forward by the sergeant so that he could use the front of his uniform to wipe the blood from his weapon.

The Mongolians then started to pillage the aid station. The last six ambulance men squatted with their hands behind their heads in front of the operating tent, guarded by another Mongolian who was obviously angry at being unable to participate in the looting. '*Wot dermo*,' he said, '*zatschem mne zdes za etimi glupymi swinjami prismatriwat. Ich wsö rawno w raschod pustjat. Lutschsche ja ich sejtschas srazu prischju?*' ('Shit, damn, why do I have to guard these stupid pigs, they'll be killed anyway. Why can't I kill them now?') '*Zakroj rot I delaj, tschto ja tebe skaschu*,' ('Shut up and do what I say') an NCO moaned back. '*Staryi chotschet eschtschö s nimi poodinotschke tschto-to soobrazit. Moschet proschtschebetschut ptischki nam eschtschö swoju pesenku I rasskaschut nam, kuda ich doblestnye prijateli smylis*.' ('The old one wants to take them to task again. Perhaps these birdies will chirp a song for us and will tell us where their heroic comrades are.')

One of the ambulance men knew a bit of Russian and understood that there were bad times ahead. 'They want to stick us like the wounded,' he whispered through his teeth. 'We've had it anyway, so I say we make a break for it at the next opportunity and try to get to the others. Our men can't be far.' 'You're right,' his neighbour said. 'I'll bump off the Ivan, then we'll run through the tent, jump over the waste pit and get into the bushes. We keep running until we're safe. It's everyone for himself, but try to keep together.'

The Mongolians were bragging loudly about their haul, especially when they reached the catering area. Excluded from the pillaging, the guard's rage steadily intensified, and most of his attention was devoted to ensuring his share of the plunder by shouts to his comrades. Then the opportunity came. As the Mongolians dug into some boxes the guard eyed them greedily and became inattentive. In a single fast movement one of the medics pulled a dagger from his boot, jumped up like a tiger, got behind the guard with one stride, and pulled him around the corner of the tent. The next moment he rammed the dagger into the Russian's kidney, turning it quickly two or three times. The Mongolian stiffened with the pain, his dull moans stifled by the Landser's hand on his mouth. The medic's comrades were already away through the tent, and he followed behind them. But they were not yet at the other end when the wounded Mongolian's cry of pain alerted the others. Machine pistols barked and bullets pattered through the sailcloth of the tent and tore down the hindmost medic with the dagger still in his hand. The others raced on and leapt wildly across the waste pit, in which tissue and human parts were heaped, single amputated limbs sticking up from the pile surrealistically. The last medic but one got caught in a tent rope as he jumped and fell headlong into the pit. The next one reached the other side, but turned back and reached out his hand to his comrade. Taking a firm grip he hauled him out of the pit, only to see him cut down by a burst of machine-gun fire in the back. Though they buzzed dangerously about him the bullets missed the other medic, who threw himself into the bushes and crawled through the undergrowth, the Mongolians' gunfire scything through the leaves and branches overhead. To his right he saw his comrades running. He rolled into a long hollow and sprinted after them.

Experienced Landsers very quickly obtained a small compass for themselves that they always kept with them, in case they should ever get separated from their comrades. Sepp, for instance, always had one in his pocket, and one of the ambulance men had one as well, which would now save the escapees' lives. Managing to avoid the enemy, they had hurried after the retreating German forces for two days before finally catching up with them. Then, after reporting the names of their slain comrades to the commanding officer, they had quietly joined the lines of marching Landsers, alone with their thoughts.

The survivors of GJR 144 managed to link up with the main fighting line, but this brought little relief. Its soldiers were at the end of their endurance. They had received no supplies for days and everybody was dirty and lousy. Ammunition for their small arms was almost exhausted and every shot had to be used sparingly. All that kept them going was the fatefulness of their situation. They knew that only order, discipline and silent forbearance of their tribulations would give them any chance of surviving their ordeal, because the only alternative was certain death at the enemy's hands.

Though it was invisible to the eyes of soldiers fighting in the front line, the commanders of the Sixth Army made a last minute attempt to prevent encirclement. The Russians had already made a deep penetration in the German line, and it was only thanks to the lack of coordination amongst their army leaders that encirclement had not yet been achieved. Fifteen German divisions were now pulled together to spearhead a push through the single remaining avenue of escape, to cross the Inhulets, get through to the Bug, and establish a new front line on its western shore. 3 GD was at the forefront of this operation and reached the Inhulets first. It managed to find a passable crossing point, and led by the pioneer battalion a load-bearing dam was built. Harassing attacks by the Soviets continued to be uncoordinated and were turned back.

The division's 138th and 144th regiments took positions to defend the bridgehead against the enemy's anticipated attack, and to ensure the passage of the divisions that were following. On 15 March 1944 heavy rain set in that finally froze and turned to an ice storm. Without any protection, exposed to the weather, bad colds spread rapidly among the chronically exhausted soldiers. Without the slightest possibility of relief from their misery, the Landsers stood in their holes tormented by fever and the shivers.

Chapter 8

The signature of a marksman

Sepp and his comrades trudged alongside a column of vehicles as the divisions gathered at the river crossing. Apathetically setting one foot before the other, they thought themselves safe from enemy attack amidst such a mass of troops.

Sepp had wrapped the telescopic sight of his gun with a piece of tenting to protect it from the icy rain. He was marching with the commanders of the 138th and 144th regiments as they discussed the defence of the river crossing with their staff. From about 30m away, there suddenly came a cry: 'Look out! The Ivans! *Taaaanks*!' At the same moment the machine gun of a T-34 clattered as it emerged from the icy rain. Everybody ran for cover, while an assault gun tried to manoeuvre into firing position. A horse was screaming shrilly in pain and fright from a gaping wound in its hindquarters. The animal belonged to the commander of GJR 138, Oberst Graf von der Goltz, who, instead of running for cover turned back to help it. At that moment a shell left the barrel of the Russian tank with a harsh flash, and seconds later a group of vehicles near the command group erupted into burning and smoking wrecks. Metal splinters buzzed and whistled through the air, and the Oberst fell to the ground as if hit by an invisible fist. The horse's innards were bloodily splashed everywhere, and it screamed just one last time before it died. Now the German assault gun fired back and hit the T-34 on the rim of its turret. With a dull explosion the tank went up in flames.

Within minutes the sudden attack was over. Sepp saw the Oberst standing up again. His right arm was missing. From his shoulder the remains of his upper arm bone stuck out like a stick. Scraps of tissue, veins and tendons were hanging from the huge wound like torn-off cables. Silently and with a look of panic in his eyes he gazed down at his right side. Seconds later the horror overwhelmed him and he slumped to the ground in blessed unconsciousness. His comrades were already there to help him.

For Sepp it was just another episode like those he experienced every day. But in Oberst von der Goltz the division had lost one of its most able commanders, who had distinguished himself not only by his above-average operational talents but also by his personal bravery. He was a very unusual and unconventional officer, who had had trouble with his chief more than once. With the mountain riflemen he had finally found a unit and a style of leadership that suited him and allowed him to utilize his abilities to best effect. He was the only regimental commander of 3 Gebirgsjäger Division who was awarded oak leaves to his Knight's Cross. It was not until some time later that Sepp learned of the Oberst's death from gangrene in a hospital in Odessa.

On 16 March the Russians intensified their attacks and involved the bridgehead held by the 138th and 144th regiments in violent battles. But the riflemen were able to defend themselves successfully. 3 GD was one of the last to withdraw across the Inhulets, and except for small rearguard actions it reached the Bug unmolested and settled in on the western shore.

During such withdrawals the tactical advantages of marksmen became clear. They kept pursuing patrols and infantry units at a safe distance and brought valuable reconnaissance back with them at the same time.

Units were particularly susceptible during a retreat, and in order to ensure the success of such manoeuvres it was necessary to keep the enemy in the dark for as long as possible. So a rearguard always remained in place until the rest of the troop had moved to its new position. Ideally this detachment would hold off enemy pursuit and then make a fighting withdrawal. This called for a high amount of self-control and courage, such as only experienced soldiers possessed. In order to have an effect on the pursuing enemy it was necessary that the rearguards' weapons should make an obvious impact, so machine gunners and marksmen were routinely utilized. Without doubt a marksman is the most effective form of infantry rearguard. In a well-camouflaged position, he awaits the enemy, observes him as long as possible to gather information about his strength and equipment, and finally forces him to the ground with two or three fast and precise shots, in which the signature of a marksman is revealed. Often the pursuing infantry did not dare to leave their positions for hours afterwards.

So Sepp usually remained behind after each overnight withdrawal to slow the Russians who came after them in the morning. He prepared his positions carefully for this, so that besides providing camouflage they also give him a certain amount of protection against bullets. But they also had to allow him to get away fast and unseen. If possible he settled down far ahead of his unit's abandoned positions, out in no-man's-land, to construct trenches and holes in readiness for his own withdrawal. If the situation allowed he constructed blast traps out of hand grenades and tripwires to cover the approaches, which enabled him to make use of the distraction caused by the explosions to either withdraw or take a couple of fast shots.

This game of resistance and withdrawal had gone on for four days now, and Sepp recognized that the Russians were getting more careful every day. Now he only took one or two shots before it seemed as if the enemy was swallowed up by the earth. On the sixth day the Soviets approached especially cautiously. They used every cover and were careful not to expose themselves. The first ones were only about 100m away before he had the opportunity for a precise shot. It must have been a reconnaissance man. He had taken position behind a bush and had stretched up amongst the foliage a bit too far. Sepp saw the unusual movement of the leaves, and looking closer he could make out parts of his body's contours. He simply aimed in the middle. He saw his hit confirmed by the violent trembling of the leaves. In tense expectation, Sepp awaited further activity by the Russians. But nothing happened. They seemed to have disappeared. After an hour he became extremely suspicious. Something was wrong. Concentrating hard, he searched the approaches without any result. In the meantime his muscles had begun to ache and he had to stretch a bit. He moved his legs. He had just put his right foot up on his left heel when he felt a heavy thump into his right heel simultaneous with the sound of a whipping bang from the Russian side. Instinctively he slid deep into his position to look at his aching foot. The whole heel of his boot was missing and there was a bloody scratch across the sole of his foot. Immediately he recognized the signature of a marksman, and he must have been a really good one judging from his shot, which was masterly.

Sepp's only thought was survival. Since the enemy had identified his position he must not show a single square centimetre of himself. He stayed deep in his hiding place as if glued to it. Obviously the Russians were not quite sure about the presumed location of the German marksman and they had not seen him hit either, so there was deadlock. None of the Soviets wanted to expose themselves to the risk of being shot, and Sepp could not see anything of his adversary despite intense observation. He hoped that the Russians would stay quiet until dusk so that he could slip away unseen. Since he had expected a quick departure from his current position he hadn't made any sanitary arrangements, and after several hours pressure began to build up in his bladder on top of all his other strains. He didn't want to pee into his pants, so using his hands he dug a hole in the ground beneath his flies without any more movement than was necessary. Into this hole he relieved himself. Peeing could be almost like an orgasm in such fearful situations.

Slowly the day passed and the fading light finally freed Sepp from his plight. As darkness fell he disappeared like a ghost along his prepared path. The next day he switched to the sector of the neighbouring company and was especially attentive. Luckily there was no sign of the Soviet marksman this time. The day after that the unit finally reached its destination.

Sepp and his comrades found well-built positions along the Bug that had been constructed during their advance two years earlier. With a bit of entrenchment work they were able to add 'comfortable' dugouts. The Russians took an amazingly long time to follow them. This misleading pause gave the Landsers about a week's rest, during which weapons, ammunition and even a few reinforcements reached them. For the riflemen this break was like a holiday. Finally they could take a long sleep, eat in comfort and see to a bit of personal hygiene. But the idyll lasted only a few days.

On the night of 25–26 March Russian storm troops crossed the Bug under cover of darkness and established a bridgehead beyond the steep bank. These hard and experienced soldiers got into the battalion's trenches in the first pale light of morning like hungry predators. With knives and sharp shovels they overpowered the surprised outposts. There was no shooting. They did not take any prisoners. An attentive machine-gun guard observing the shore with his binoculars from about 200m saw Russians on something like a raft in the pale morning fog, and then he looked at the German forward positions more by chance. There he saw two Russian helmets for a fraction of a second, momentarily revealed above the trench's edge.

Then there came shots and the rattle of sub-machine guns. Screams became audible. The beginnings of the Russian attack had finally been noticed and violent close combat broke out among the trenches. Within seconds all the riflemen were awake, had their weapons in their hands and had moved into their positions. Then the Russians attacked them across the river. In boats and on rafts, they came across the water without any regard for the deadly German defensive fire. Since the Russians attacked without the support of artillery the defenders had all the advantages on their side in their well-built trenches. While it took little effort to control the assault coming across the river, a threatening situation was developing in the trenches attacked by the Russian storm troops who had crossed overnight. One sector after another fell into their hands. So the Germans quickly formed a task force to mount a counterstrike. This managed to prevent the enemy from making any further gains, but the Russians defended the positions they had already captured doggedly. While Sepp put one shot after another into the Russians attacking across the river, a sergeant looked through his binoculars into the Russian-held trenches. Through these he observed a soldier in a white fur hat, obviously the group's leader since he could always be seen at the heart of the fighting, encouraging his men to violent resistance. The sergeant touched Sepp's shoulder: 'I think the fine hat over there is their leader. If you do him our comrades will get the Ivans.' Sepp knew about the motivation provided by officers fighting in the front line and the demoralizing effect if they fell. In two steps he was alongside the sergeant and had found a good place to rest his rifle, with a clear field of fire towards the occupied trench. To ensure killing his enemy he loaded one of his valuable explosive bullets, which were only rarely found amongst captured Russian ammunition.

With his gun in a firm firing position he awaited his opportunity for a lethal shot. The sergeant acted as his observer now. He could scan the entire trench with his binoculars, while Sepp only got a limited view through his telescopic sight. Suddenly the fur hat appeared again above the trench's edge. 'Sepp, over there,' the sergeant called. The rifle swung round, but the target was gone again. Now the observer proved himself, having recognized the direction of the Russian's movement. 'Sepp, he's running right. Go with him. Do you see part of his hat above the edge?' Now Sepp had picked up the rhythm of his opponent's movement. He would appear at a junction next, the only possibility Sepp would get for an aimed shot at the moment. Sepp shifted his weapon, taking the small piece of trench into the reticle. He waited for the decisive moment. Then suddenly the fur hat was visible in the telescopic sight. The shot whipped over the distance of 120m in the fraction of a second and struck. Sepp and the sergeant saw the fur hat puff up like a balloon and then burst bloodily like an overripe melon.

Without their leader the Russians became confused and disoriented. Taking advantage of this, the riflemen stormed into the occupied trench and in violent close combat managed to kill all the invaders.

After this shot Sepp immediately turned his attention back to the Russians coming across the river. His observer also took up his carbine again. The strength of the marksman was now fast and very accurate fire. Since the attackers on the rafts made very easy targets, they jumped into the water long before reaching the shore in order to escape the annihilating German fire. For the marksman it was like target practice as he picked off the heads bobbing in the water. Since the Russians continued their attack without any regard for losses the river became a hideous bloodbath. After few hours it looked like the sewer of a slaughterhouse. Bloody grey bilgewater loaded with corpses, torn off limbs and bits of tissue flowed down towards the Black Sea.

The regiment managed to successfully beat off all attacks and to maintain its positions. But in neighbouring sectors the Soviets broke through the German defences. The 144th nevertheless held its ground until 27 March despite its exposed flank.

During the night of 27–28 March the regiment finally started its withdrawal towards the Dniester. Three hundred kilometres had to be covered on foot. To reduced the pressure of the Russian pursuit the division tried to put a greater distance between them by a forty-eight-hour forced march. But it is one of the basic rules of war that a fleeing enemy should never be allowed to get any rest, and the Russians had learned this lesson during the earlier years of the conflict. Despite the strain of keeping up, their pressure on the withdrawing riflemen did not slacken in any way.

To top it all 3 GD's supply lines collapsed. No ammunition, no food and no anti-tank weapons reached it. The last lorry theoretically carrying food brought two tons of plain chocolate and 500 Iron Crosses Second Class – one of those strange situations when a Landser seriously asked himself who the organizational geniuses were that worked in the logistics branch. So the riflemen lived on half a chocolate bar and ships' biscuits for days. This combination was rich in roughage and gave them bad constipation – which was a nice change from the usual diarrhoea.

So the forced march of two days did not bring the relief that had been hoped for. The Russians managed to keep their vanguard at the enemy's heels and their main forces came on right behind them. The withdrawal of the division became a running battle without any real front line. The Soviets were everywhere again. Individual pockets of German resistance formed, which fought on in isolation as again and again they tried to unite into a more substantial fighting force.

The Russian infantry began to adopt a new tactic: they now had armoured half-tracks, which could transport them right into the fighting zone. These could only be fought with anti-tank guns, but with the exception of hand grenades the riflemen did not have even the simplest such weapons. So the full force of the protected Russian infantry hit them.

With droning motors and the rattle of tracks a dozen such half-track vehicles headed for the Landsers' positions. Feverishly they thought of ways to try to counter this new danger, since the Russian infantry's ability to immediately disembark rendered the riflemen's usual anti-tank tactic using hand grenades obsolete. Sepp observed the approaching vehicles through his binoculars, searching for a weak spot. There, through a vision slit in the armoured front plate covering the cab, he saw a movement: the driver. A gap of 10cm by 30cm, and 80m away. The chance of hitting him was low, but it provided the only possibility of stopping such a vehicle with a simple bullet from a gun. Sepp paid close attention as the vehicle came on at a walking speed in order to cope with sudden undulations in the ground. He loaded an explosive bullet and rolled a tent square to support his rifle. He got the gun into firing position and took aim. As he had practised a hundred times, he breathed regularly and quietly despite the extreme strain. The sight settled on its target, and his right forefinger took the pressure point of the trigger, all his senses keyed to their highest pitch. The half-track was about 60m away and for a brief moment he could see the eyes of the driver through the slit. The shot crashed out only seconds later – and found its target. Immediately the vehicle slewed off course and slithered into a grenade crater, where it got stuck with its tracks spinning. Panicking, the Russian soldiers jumped from their wrecked vehicle and were immediately subjected to German infantry fire that prevented them from pushing further ahead. Obviously there was just one driver in the cabin, and it seemed he was separated from the fighting compartment, so nobody could get to the steering wheel once the driver was shot. The Achilles' heel had been found, and with it came some hope that they could reduce the danger. Using his last twenty explosive bullets Sepp managed to knock out seven of the twelve attacking vehicles by killing or wounding the drivers. The remaining five broke through the riflemen's position and unloaded their troops, but the Landsers managed to destroy them in hard-fought close combat.

Though the Russian attack was successfully withstood here, the positions of neighbouring divisions were again penetrated at many points. Another withdrawal was therefore necessitated in order to create a new defensive line.

Amazingly the army commanders at OKH managed to bring in Romanian bombers and a detachment of anti-tank guns to relieve the pressure; these provided the necessary breathing space to establish a new front line by destroying twenty-four Russian tanks. After fighting without air support for months their own planes seemed unreal to the Landsers. In spite of this the ground attack remained the main focus of action and 3 GD once again managed to hold its sector – at the cost of a third of its personnel. Failing here, the Russians switched their attack to a weaker point in the German lines. While just a few kilometres away a fresh unit was ground down by the Russian attack and hundreds of young soldiers died screaming, the riflemen of GJR 144 even managed to sleep for a bit in the sudden tranquillity of their own sector.

Chapter 9

The excesses of human violence

Spearheaded by a strong force of tanks the Russian breakthrough finally succeeded on 2 April 1944. Immediate escape from the deadly Russian embrace became necessary even for 3 Gebirgsjäger Division – an extremely risky operation, since its troops were equipped with only small arms and hand grenades. But a sudden onset of bad weather provided a welcome ally. In the evening of that day a violent snowstorm began. Vision was reduced to less than 50m. The division's few survivors left their positions and marched off in long lines, which wound away into the infinity of the falling snow like worms. As always in such withdrawals, that brought only misery, the wounded were those who suffered most. Everyone who was fairly mobile dragged himself along with the help of his comrades, fear of death through Russian mistreatment mobilizing the last reserves of their energy. Those who could not be moved had to be left behind. These resigned themselves to the certainty of a speedy death. Many asked for a gun in order to end their own lives.

In the silent pain of parting, comrades of hard battles looked into the sadness of each other's eyes one last time, promising to pass messages on to their families or handing over cherished keepsakes to be taken home to their loved ones. Needless to say, many of these pictures and amulets and other unspectacular but valued mementoes never reached their intended recipients, being soon afterwards destroyed in explosions or soiled beyond recognition by dirt and blood.

A last handshake of mutual understanding, then the snowstorm swallowed up the abandoned men.

A few minutes after the riflemen had left their positions, dull shots echoed through the darkness behind them as some of the wounded sought a merciful release from their misery. Many riflemen started almost imperceptibly, but the pain remained, buried deep inside, beyond the thick shell of outer indifference.

As usual Sepp had wrapped his marksman's rifle in a tent square and hung it on his back, and was carrying an MP40 ready to hand on his breast. He safeguarded the flank of his marching group with some comrades. They had been walking for about an hour when he heard scraps of conversation and the sound of marching. A sense of relief welled up inside him – there were some comrades between them and the enemy. But minutes later it shot through him like an electric shock: Russian words were now clearly audible, and shadows could be seen through the snow less than 10m away. They were marching parallel to a Russian convoy! 'Don't lose your nerve, now,' he thought. If fighting had broken out it would have been the end of them. Sepp tapped his comrades and signalled to them with his eyes. It was enough. A silent warning sped down the German column and everybody understood at once. Not a word was spoken, and slowly they moved away from the Russian troop.

But in the early morning hours, while it was still dark, they came to a Russian-held road that lay across their line of march, conveying a never-ending stream of men and material. After an hour of nerve-wracking hesitation they decided to fight their way over the road. When a transport convoy came along the riflemen stormed from the bushes at the roadside and forced their way across in a short but violent firefight. Sepp went first with four comrades. Using a gap of about 40m between two vehicles they jumped from the bushes a few metres in front of a lorry. While three riflemen emptied the magazines of their MP40s into the driver's cab, Sepp and his other companion threw two hand grenades each into the cargo space. The front wheels of the lorry turned, and accompanied by the dull crash of the hand grenades it veered into the roadside ditch. Its cab door opened and in the pale light of the burning truck the driver's face appeared for a moment, bloody and distorted. Gurgling, a big splash of blood shot from his mouth before he toppled to the snow-covered ground like a felled tree. While the five riflemen fired at the next lorry the rest of the regiment hurried across the road. In a few minutes the whole affair was over and darkness had swallowed the riflemen as if they were ghosts.

The remnants of the division managed to reform, but it was found that their withdrawal was too late. They were near the town of

Bakalovo, 25km from the mouth of the Kuchurgan, a natural barrier. In a fast and brave thrust Russian tank units had already taken the city and encircled five German divisions, 3 GD among them. All these units were in a desperate condition. Battalions had been reduced to half their fighting strength, and they had only light infantry weapons and hand grenades. The Landsers were hungry and at the end of their physical strength. But their fear of falling into Russian hands prevented any thought of surrender. As the highest-ranking officer the commander of 3 GD, General Wittmann, took command of the entire German force. His decision was to burst through the deadly encirclement and link up with the German positions on the western shore of the Kuchurgan.

The escape bid had to be mounted energetically and immediately, but in addition to their dire logistical situation the Germans' entire radio network had also collapsed, so communication was only possible by means of runners. This resulted in much valuable time being wasted. By the time preparations for the breakout were finalized it was already late afternoon on 5 April.

At 17:00 3 GD lined up as the advance guard. The Russians were obviously surprised by the determination of these exhausted troops, and they hardly resisted, so that by 21:00 Bakalovo had been taken. GJR 144 was in a little village 2km from the town.

In addition to the five divisions under General Wittmann it emerged that XXIV Army Corps had been surrounded in a neighbouring valley, and in order to give as much weight as possible to the German offensive the two commanders agreed on a simultaneous breakout. But the attempt to orchestrate their attacks failed because of their difficulties communicating with each other. Finally contact between the two forces broke down completely. General Wittmann had rightly feared that the escape of the army corps would go too slowly and now it seemed to have stalled. Restoring contact between their forces was vital for their mutual survival, so Wittmann interrupted his own operations and ordered his units to wait around Bakalovo. In order to relieve pressure on the neighbouring valley he exposed his own troops to increasing and more co-ordinated Russian attacks.

GJR 144 was hit especially hard. Amidst the burning houses of the occupied village Cossack cavalry attacked them all night. Sepp and ten of his comrades had settled in the ruins of a farm. With practised skill, he prepared four positions with good cover and a clear field of fire, taking special care to allow for the possibility of fast and concealed changes of position.

There was a ghostlike aesthetic quality to the appearance of the first Cossack company, which galloped out of the red twilight of the burning fires at 21:30. The riders were highly skilled in the use of their horses and in no time they were inside the German positions. It was almost impossible to shoot the riders in the flickering light, so the Germans targeted their horses instead. From occasional shots at Russian transport horses Sepp knew which zones to aim at. If the bullet hit the breastbone the horse fell immediately, overturning and often trapping its rider. If the hit was in the intestines or kidney area the animal started to buck furiously, became uncontrollable and finally broke down and died slowly, beating with its legs violently and convulsively. Depending on the Cossacks' distance from the German positions, Sepp shot into the breastbone of the foremost animals, and into the soft parts of those that were further away. His comrades then shot at the downed riders. In this way they managed to fend off several attacks. After an hour the approaches were filled with dying animals, innocent victims of the excesses of human violence. An increasing revulsion of being forced to shoot these poor animals arose within Sepp.

The fight escalated into a wild battle. A Cossack suddenly appeared about 50m in front of Sepp's position. He swung his gun round and fired into the horse's breast, but just as he pulled the trigger the horse jumped over a corpse. Because of this the bullet hit its abdominal wall and tore it open for half the length of its belly. The horse's intestines slipped out, and the horse stepped on them, pulling them out even further. Mute in sudden fear of death, which showed in its wide eyes that were as big as fried eggs, it stood there with trembling flanks, its rider turned to stone on its back. To Sepp it seemed that the animal stared at him for minutes on end with a look of unspeakable depth and sadness, asking for the meaning of its absurd approaching death. But in reality just seconds elapsed before Sepp put the creature out of its misery with a headshot. A machine-pistol salvo shattered the breast of the Cossack still sitting on the back of the dying horse.

The next wave of horsemen succeeded in forcing its way into the village and violent close combats broke out. Sepp had hidden his marksman's gun again and fought with his MP40 alongside a group of seven men who had hidden in the ruins of the farm. Their situation seemed more hopeless every minute. Suddenly the howling sound of multiple rocket launchers gave them just seconds to duck down into the supposed safety of the ruins. The roaring barrage came down right between the Cossacks and riflemen, and ironically it was the Russian horsemen who were hit hardest. Bits of horses and riders mixed with lumps of earth and debris rained down. Explosions and screams of death were all round them, the apocalyptic thunder now being joined by German artillery fire.

Both sides had attempted to support their men without really knowing the fighting situation or the positions of their soldiers. The rocket and artillery fire lasted only a few minutes, but it destroyed an entire Cossack battalion and killed several riflemen and resulted in a short break in the battle, an eerie silence before the next wave of the enemy came rushing up.

The makeshift positions of the regiment and the insufficiency of its weapons and equipment resulted in huge losses. In the few hours of this defensive battle GJR 144 alone lost almost 300 men, 168 of them wounded. All contact with the division was lost. Patrols failed to get through because of the Russian lines that had been established in the meantime. The regiment's very existence was now seriously threatened. In this extremely tricky situation its commander, Oberst Lorch, decided on the only practical solution. Only an immediate breakout would give them any chance of rejoining the division.

What is described as a small local action in army reports and divisional histories invariably meant hundredfold misery for the wounded that had to be left behind. The medical logistics always collapsed under such circumstances. The route between the front line and the main aid station was disrupted by loss of vehicles, petrol and personnel far more than was the road from the hinterland to the front, especially when the fighting situation was as confused as it was during a withdrawal.

The companies were advised of Oberst Lorch's plan by runners. The few doctors and ambulance men then triaged the wounded, and where requested the wounded who were to be left behind were given guns. These preparations proceeded rapidly and without any room for sentimentality. The relentlessness of war obliged everybody to obey its merciless rules: to inflict death and to bear it were equally natural.

The determined attack began at dawn. Realizing the seriousness of the situation the riflemen mobilized the last reserves of their strength and threw themselves into the fight, managing to free themselves from the deadly encirclement.

The subsequent official reports talked of an heroic and meticulously planned operation. But the reality was a confused mess that only succeeded thanks to a good share of luck. Many soldiers lost their nerve. Their fight became escape, escape became panic. Just before the decisive attack Sepp stood at one of the last field kitchens with a group of comrades, filling his water bottle with hot tea, when suddenly the dull drone of motors and the rattling of tracks drifted down the wind towards them from out of the morning haze. Immediately they were spurred into action. Their senses taut, they peered in the direction of the noise. Nothing was visible, but suddenly a call rang out: 'Ivan is through – *taaanks*!' The riflemen ran. The cook jumped on to his field kitchen, whipped up his horses and disappeared, tea sloshing from the still-open containers. The more experienced riflemen tried to prevent a rout, bringing some Landsers back to their senses by kicks and slaps around the ears. But almost half of them had disappeared in the same direction as the field kitchen. Those who remained trembled as they awaited the Russian tanks, which emerged out of the haze minutes later – and turned out to be German assault guns that had come to support them! It took half an hour to collect the panicked soldiers together again. Boxes round the ears and kicks in the pants were deemed more effective than expensive disciplinary measures right now. There was even room for cynical humour. Among the stalwarts who had stood their ground Sepp recognized a sergeant-major with many decorations – it was the Viking with the huge red moustache who had comforted him after his first hit and had offered him booze. He had come through the whole operation with stoic calm and had kept his men at it relentlessly. While the others formed up again he remarked in his special way, dry like a fart: 'Boys, did you know that there'll be no pay any more?' There was uncomprehending silence all around him. 'In future there will be just *Fersengeld*!' – which means literally 'to give heels money', a German expression for turning tail. And with that he roared with laughter. He was a guy Sepp would remember again and again.

Around noon the field reserve battalion of the regiment north-west of Bakalovo met opposition of a special kind. Extraordinarily precise gunfire came towards them from a forest. Within minutes eleven Landsers of the leading company had been brought down by head and chest shots. The cry 'Snipers!' went up, and everybody pressed into cover as well as they could. Two company leaders who raised their heads from cover to look through their binoculars paid with their lives. Russian explosive bullets shattered their skulls. The huge number of hits made only one conclusion plausible: there had to be a whole company of marksmen before them. The riflemen had only heard of such things, and had only ever encountered single Russian marksmen until now. Without artillery or heavy mortars they were helpless. The fire came from the impenetrable green of the conifers. Machine-gun salvos in that general direction were without any visible effect and were answered by accurate fire that proved deadly to those machine gunners who exposed themselves. As carefully as possible the riflemen withdrew into protected positions, the damaged buildings of a *kolkhoz* (a Soviet collective farm) providing them with cover. Then a runner was sent to report the situation to regimental headquarters. The battalion was hoping that heavy weapons would be able to bombard the forest, but the combat situation and the lack of artillery rendered such a conventional solution impossible.

Sepp was by now recognized throughout the regiment as an intelligent and successful marksman who was also known to the regiment's commander. So Oberst Lorch, though he seems to have regarded the Russian opposition as token resistance, gave a written order to the runner that he should take to the command dugout of II Battalion. It ordered Marksman Allerberger to fight an entire company of Russian snipers. Three hours later Sepp was inside the ruined farm buildings being apprised of the situation.

The forest lay about 300m from the *kolkhoz*. To spot any Russians in the thick woods Sepp had to get nearer and make them fire a shot. For that he had to present them with a target. He therefore filled five grenade bags with grass, put helmets on them, and with a charred piece of wood drew in eyes, a nose and a mouth. He always kept the cloth-less frame of an umbrella with him, to which grass and branches were now attached, leaving just one small hole in the centre to look through. A hundred metres from the farm buildings there was a small hollow with bushes along the edge, an ideal observation position that he could reach by crawling without being seen by the enemy. He arranged a signal by which the other riflemen would know when to carefully reveal the target 'heads' in different positions amongst the ruins. Some twenty minutes later Sepp reached his observation position and carefully set his camouflage umbrella in place so that his movements would not attract attention. Then he attentively scanned the Russian positions for possible locations that might conceal marksmen. Analyzing the hits they had scored up to now indicated that the Russians had a good view of the Germans, so they must have elevated positions, logically among the thick treetops. But Sepp could hardly imagine that experienced marksmen could make such a cardinal error, shooting from a tree without any possibility of withdrawing safely or taking cover. He gave the arranged signal and his comrades showed the artificial heads. Suddenly there were several shots from the Russian side and he saw branches move from the pressure waves of their fire.

Sepp set off back to the *kolkhoz* immediately, where he discussed his plan with the sergeant who had assumed command of the company after the death of its two officers. Sepp placed five machine guns in well-hidden positions with a good field of fire in the direction of the forest, and relocated the soldiers in charge of the fake heads. Slightly to one side he chose a well-camouflaged position for himself. Then he signalled to the riflemen to raise the artificial heads from cover while he observed the Russian line. When a head was shot, he could make out the marksman's position. Then while the machine guns fired into the treetop Sepp put in his aimed shots. This way he could camouflage his fire for as long as possible and conceal the presence of a German marksman from the Russians. The fact that the Soviet snipers had shot for their enemies' heads five times but were sitting in the trees proved to Sepp that they were good shots, but tactically inexperienced. This reduced his fear of the upcoming duel against their superior numbers.

His plan worked with almost frightening efficiency. When a 'head' appeared, one, two or sometimes even three Russians shot at it at the same time. Sepp located the moving branches, took aim, waited for the MG salvo, fired, and hit one target after another. The hit Russians fell from the trees like sacks. A quick change of positions, and the game started all over again. Within an hour he had shot eighteen enemy snipers this way. Then suddenly the fire on the artificial heads stopped. It was 17:00, and since there had been no shots from the forest for about an hour the sergeant decided to advance into the

1. Allerberger and a Selbstladegewehr (self-loading rifle) Model 43 with telescopic sight, 20 April 1945. This semi-automatic carbine was a very favourable advance with some of the recoil energy when fired being diverted to the reloading function.

2. Obergefreiter Josef 'Sepp' Allerberger.

3. The concept: a Wehrmacht propaganda photo of a Gebirgsjäger sniper.

4. Most successful Wehrmacht sniper Obergefreiter Mathias Hetzenauer was also attached to 3.G.D. The weapon he holds is the K98k standard carbine with side mounted Zeiss Zielsechs telescopic sight.

5. Generalfeldmarschall Ferdinand Schörner. A man of considerable personal valour, he was noted as a ruthless disciplinarian, although this may have been because he was always placed in the most difficult situations where his loyalty to the Nazi cause ensured that he obeyed his orders to the letter.

. Major Kloss, commander G.J.R. 144./3.G.D., fell 10 November 1944.

7. General Paul Klatt, commander 3.G.D.

8. Difficult terrain in eastern Czechoslovakia for Schörner's final resistance to the Soviets.

9. Poorly equipped German mountain troops pass through a rail marshalling yard during the long retreat.

woods. Sepp and an MG provided cover. The company reached the forest without coming under fire, and it became obvious that the enemy had withdrawn. The sergeant waved over to Sepp and the others. Carefully, mistrusting the deceptive silence, he approached the forest and saw young women lying dead in the grass before him.

This massive deployment of marksmen was a special Russian tactic that, amazingly, owed its origins to German influence.

In the 1920s the two former enemies had got together in a marriage of convenience. Russia had been brought to its knees technologically and economically by the turmoil of revolution, while Germany was not allowed to develop military equipment by the terms of the Versailles Treaty. Although they were political opponents, their governments made a virtue of necessity. The Germans provided Russia with technical know-how and industrial equipment and in exchange were allowed to develop and test their new military machines in Russia. In the development of fighting vehicles and aircraft in particular there was close co-operation. As part of the deal that was viewed as being of insignificant importance at the time Germany also provided the Russians with the technological and tactical expertise to construct an efficient telescopic sight and improve Russian marksmanship. The Russians had not used telescopic sights up to that point.

While the Wehrmacht thereafter relied on a highly mobile war of movement and neglected proper development of infantry weapons and tactics, the young Soviet army, because of its limited means, concentrated on the latter. Examples of their innovative developments were self-loading guns, anti-tank weapons and the multi-barrel mortar. And while the German Army continued to use old pre-war telescopic sights until 1940, the Red Army developed modern sniper weapons and made use of extensive numbers of marksmen. These operated alone, as sniper and observer teams or pairs of snipers who worked together, and in entire troops of up to sixty marksmen.

From the very beginning of the Russian campaign the Soviets had inflicted considerable losses on the approaching Wehrmacht, especially amongst its officers and leaders. Often they managed to halt the German advance for days without any heavy weapons. In the euphoria of their victories during the opening months of the campaign the Germans wrote off the marksmen as insidious snipers and ignored the latent danger they represented. But in 1942, with the onset of more static warfare and defensive actions the problem became more obvious and urgent. The lack of telescopic sights in the German Army was now critical. The introduction of a telescopic sight with a magnification of only about 1.5x was utterly inadequate for precise long-distance shots.

Until regular production of more powerful telescopic sights could begin ways had to be found to improvise. Captured weapons such as Sepp's were pressed into service, and hunting weapons with telescopic sights were gathered up in Germany and sent to the front. The few marksmen's rifles available from barracks back home and in the possession of the police were brought together and provided the first equipment of the Wehrmacht's marksmen. Guidelines on telescopic-sighted guns and the deployment of marksmen initially appeared at the end of 1942, but the first official instructions were not issued until May 1943.

Back in the forest, there were sudden shots as Sepp's comrades gathered the weapons and ammunition of the women who had been shot from the treetops.

One young woman, not yet in her twenties, was lying face down across her rifle, and one of the riflemen had reached down and rolled her apparently lifeless body over to get to the gun. Her right hand was inside her blood-soaked uniform jacket, in which a bullet hole gaped right between her breasts. Bloody foam was on her lips. When the rifleman bent over to pick up the rifle she suddenly pulled a Tokarev automatic pistol from her jacket, gurgled '*Smert Faschistam!*' ('Death to the Fascists!'), and pulled the trigger. Alerted by her movement, the rifleman jumped aside so that the shot only nicked his backside, leaving a bloody stripe across his trousers. As he jumped back the Landser swung round his MP40 and pulled the trigger. Dully smacking, the bullets went right into the dying Russian's chest. She writhed again as if electrified and her features hardened in death.

It was the first time the riflemen present had knowingly fought against women. Now that they stood before the lifeless bodies and saw the broken young faces they all experienced a strange feeling of revulsion and shame, even though they knew that in the end there was no way to avoid the law of kill or be killed. If they had known that their enemies were girls they might have fought with less vehemence and in consequence have become victims of their own morality.

At dawn the following day the Russian lines were broken and the division pushed its way through, but it took hours for individual units and scattered groups to get back to the main body. Sepp's battalion, which had been reduced to sixty men, was one of these. As ever during their withdrawals they tried to leave nothing but scorched earth and a destroyed infrastructure to the enemy, and German engineers therefore prepared to blow up a railway tunnel that was an important escape route for the soldiers pouring back from the front. When II Battalion had emerged from the tunnel Captain Kloss told the leader of the engineers that another detachment of engineers was following as the rearguard and he should delay demolition until they had passed through the tunnel. But the engineer officer's nerves were shattered and he detonated the charges less than ten minutes later. After another ten minutes just two dirty and disillusioned engineers from the rearguard caught up with the rest of the battalion and reported that the tunnel had exploded at the very moment they were passing through it. These two men had survived only because they had been the vanguard of the detachment. Rage spread. Many thought about the futility and increasing madness of this war. But what could a single soldier do about it? Survival was all that mattered now.

They continued on their way and after an hour reached the agreed rendezvous place. A guard suddenly called out to them: 'Halt! What's the password?' 'What password, arsehole?' a rifleman in the vanguard called back. 'Where would we get it from anyway? Stick your password in your penis.' And with that he continued on his way. The Landsers behind him stiffened in disbelief when suddenly a machine gun barked and the volley blew the Landser's chest apart, blood splashing everywhere. Within seconds they had all dived for cover. Captain Kloss crawled forward and screamed: 'Stop firing, arsehole! This is II Battalion. Get your chief now!' Some minutes later a lieutenant called out questions that Kloss answered bad-temperedly. Finally Kloss was asked to come forward alone. He got up carefully and went towards the guard post with his gun held out. He was full of rage about the death of the soldier and the loss of his pioneers. Now the lieutenant got up too. At his feet the guard lay behind his machine gun looking up. It was a lad, trembling in fear. His voice cracking in fury, Kloss screamed at him: 'You fucking dirtbag, you've shot a comrade! I'll finish you off, you swine, I'll put a bullet through your head!' He worked himself up into a rage more and more, and finally lost control. With a long scream he suddenly emptied the whole magazine of his pistol into the defenceless soldier staring up at him wide eyed. Then some of the Landsers threw themselves on their commander and forced him to the ground, slapping his face to force him to calm down. Except for his own men and the lieutenant, who showed understanding for the captain's nervous breakdown, there were no witnesses to this incident, so it passed without consequence, a testament to the increasingly aberrant and arbitrary nature of military discipline. But the standard message that would have been sent to the families of the two dead soldiers, 'Died for Grossdeutschland', had a more than bitter aftertaste here.

The regiment was now finally able to get into radio contact with the rest of Wittmann's fighting group, enabling the attack of the five divisions to be coordinated for the next phase of the breakout. As the new day dawned they managed to burst through the last ring of the deadly Russian embrace. But the German front itself was by now in an alarming condition. Wittmann's command was entirely isolated. Patrols sent out in all directions encountered only enemy forces. In their own reconnaissance sorties the marksmen always brought back valuable information.

The marksmen were directly under the orders of their company commanders and were excused from regular duties. From them they received their orders to fight or go out on reconnaissance. Because their survival depended on being unseen by the enemy, experienced marksmen developed the ability to move discreetly. Exotic camouflage such as was advocated in training manuals and was shown in propaganda film and photographs hardly played any part. Complete camouflage was very time-consuming and rendered the soldier immobile. In the extremely fluid and erratic situation on the Eastern Front there was hardly ever sufficient breathing space to adopt such measures. Every marksman, as long as he had survived his first few weeks in this role, created his own improvised camouflaging measures that could be deployed quickly, were easy to transport, and compromised his mobility as little as possible. So as already mentioned, Sepp had got hold of an old umbrella that he shortened and removed the cloth from so that he could weave twigs and grass into its wire frame. When not required, this little camouflage umbrella was easy to fold up and could be carried amongst his fighting kit without difficulty.

It was on the evening of 6 April 1944 that radio contact with neighbouring units of Combat Group Wittmann was finally restored. The news that was received painted a dark picture of disintegration. Every unit was involved in fighting isolated actions. Withdrawal and reconsolidation of the front line was absolutely vital. The Nazi propaganda machine invented a good name for this: 'elastic warfare'.

At about 22:00 General Wittmann's command post received repeated radio messages from 97 Jäger Division. All units in the area were asked to withdraw to a new front line beyond the Kuchurgan. 97 JG had prepared crossing points and would make them safe with support from 257 Infantry Division. It was high time, because the Russians were pursuing them energetically and throwing more and more shells at them. The combat group's last heavy guns were therefore massed and commenced a barrage against the Russians attempting to bolt their route of escape. While the Russians were still surprised by the bombardment the German infantry units set out. But the Russians reacted quickly, transferring part of their available forces to the breakout zone and subjecting the riflemen to an annihilating fire. But experienced soldiers and sergeants urged the riflemen into a frenzied attack. They threw themselves into the fight like cats, leaping boldly from cover to cover and shooting from the hip as they stormed the enemy positions. The marksmen hung back a little and fired between their comrades, concentrating as well as they could on the Russian machine gunners and mortar positions. For an hour the fight raged before their enemies' courage failed, and then Combat Group Wittmann stormed through the breach as fast as was possible. A moonless night helped them and protected them from any further major Russian attacks. Skirmishes with enemy patrols they could cope with. At 09:00 on 7 April the group reached the Kuchurgan and immediately ferried across it. The group's five divisions by now consisted of about 4,500 soldiers, 3 GD having been denuded to less than a thousand. Without halting they went on to the Dniester, which they crossed three days later.

It was a fateful crossing, because they were leaving Russian territory and entering the Bessarabia region of Romania. After three years of severe fighting and shocking losses the Russian campaign had finally failed. It became clear to the riflemen that the war was now approaching their homeland. It was not about conquering any more: now it was about putting off the relentless vengeance of the enemy for as long as a scrap of hope remained of somehow preventing it.

Chapter 10

Worse than hungry foxes

The German forces now regrouped, integrating Romanian units into their ranks. But the fighting force of their Romanian allies was so low, because of their lack of experience and equipment, that they brought no lasting relief. 3 Gebirgsjäger Division was in a very bad state once again as regards personnel and equipment and could only repair some of the damage by absorbing the scattered units and equipment of dispersed divisions. In addition more than a third of 3 GD was transferred just ten days later, on 17 April, to support a seriously endangered section of the front, where it was placed under the command of the divisions already posted there. Sepp was lucky to remain with the rest of the division, because what was designated 'Combat Group Rhode' (Kdr. GJR 138) – of which GJR 138 was the principal element – subsequently sustained awful losses of more than 800 men.

Fate was kind to the rest of the division for a few weeks. May showed itself from its best angle as regards the weather, and in GJR 144's sector of the front, on the banks of the Dniester, the war seemed to take a break. Their opponents were entrenched within firing range but limited themselves to a 'loose' static fight – which means that they exchanged occasional mortar and machine-gun fire and to relieve the boredom sent out small patrols from time to time. The river between the adversaries was about 300 or 400m wide, and it wasn't possible for the marksmen to creep between the enemy lines and search out good shooting positions. So Sepp toured the positions of his unit daily and confined himself to shooting at special targets pointed out by his comrades. At distances of up to 400m it was art more than accuracy if he managed to hit a head. But logically, he calculated, the demoralizing effect on those who escaped his projectiles by a hair's breadth when they thought themselves at a safe distance would be considerable.

The daily routine of warfare seemed to diffuse a soldier's sense of danger. As a rule he could not look upon his enemy's fire as a direct and personal threat. Only if he was targeted by a single weapon or was involved in single combat man to man did he get the feeling of individual menace again, the feeling that 'they're out to get me'. Selective shooting by invisible marksmen scared even the most experienced soldiers. The marksman represented an individualized threat to his life. This explains the amazing impact of such soldiers on the battlefield, where, for example, a single marksman could drive an entire company into cover for hours. They would be seized by a kind of psychological paralysis, in which every single man felt individually threatened and feared that the slightest movement would make him the shooter's next victim.

Generally a soldier has to live with the constant awareness of his own vulnerability and potential death. Many fail to bear up under this psychological load and in action they panic. This showed itself in wild and unaimed shooting and a latent readiness to run away that became uncontrollable as soon as the enemy got closer or the soldier found himself apparently alone. So resistance to stress is more significant to the quality of a soldier than his shooting skill or technical expertise. Good marksmen are therefore hard to find in peacetime, and the selection and training of future marksmen based on no more than their shooting skills has to be considered a serious mistake. Above all a marksman has to have a high degree of self-control and strong nerves. Shooting can be learned, particularly as the shooting skills of marksmen are overrated in a military context. The reality of service in the field showed that shooting distances for small arms were 400m at most, and usually below 200m, and if the marksman aimed at the middle of the largest surface a hit became almost certain. Absolute reliability, methodical routine and sure hits made a marksman, not artistic shots from hundreds of metres away. Such long-distance shots were more like a party trick, if they were successful at all.

Sepp made his usual tour through the positions. For days there had been just insignificant skirmishes with the Russians, who did not dare to leave their positions because they knew there was an expert marksman around. He had spent the whole morning with different machine-gun guards and observed the enemy lines without finding a target. In the afternoon he decided to visit the battalion's northern positions, which he rarely visited because they lay in a very wide curve of the river so that the Russian positions were more than a kilometre away. No fighting was taking place here apart from occasional and unaimed MG fire, and the distance was far too great for a rifle shot.

Among his comrades there was a holiday-like mood. They were enjoying the warm weather, sprawling in the sun shirtless, cracking lice. Some had a wash, using the lid of their mess kit as a bowl. Aesthetes even tried to scratch the skid marks or dried diarrhoea from their underpants, that had not been washed for weeks, and the heavy, spicy smell of rotten cheese from socks that had been put out to air hung over the whole scene. The mood was so relaxed that Sepp was invited to join in a delicious impromptu snack of hard cookies with artificial marmalade from a tin and ersatz coffee. These luxuries had been liberated by the company scrounger the previous day, from the jeep of two artillery officers making a brief exploratory reconnaissance.

As the riflemen chatted, a machine-gun guard who had just been relieved told them about strange sounds coming over from the Russian side of the river. He described them as being like the background noise you hear around a swimming pool. This made Sepp curious, and he decided to investigate.

Between their positions and the neighbouring company there was a piece of unoccupied ground from which he hoped to get a clear view into the Russian positions. After he had gone about 500m he found a bushy hill with enough cover to make his observation.

Carefully he crawled through the high grass between two bushes, and before him was an astonishing scene. Invisible from the German positions, a small bay in the riverbank was full of Russians enjoying assorted bathing activities. They were obviously feeling very safe – nobody was guarding them or protecting them. Sepp guessed the distance at about 600m. There was no wind and the air was dry. In a mixture of jealous rage at their carelessness, personal ambition to score a hit at this range, and realization that it was essential to show determination to the enemy at every opportunity, the decision to take a shot across this huge distance welled up inside him. He chose a large, very static target. On the embankment of the opposite shore some Russians were lying together sunbathing on the sand. Since Sepp was in an elevated shooting position the soldiers he aimed for presented an almost right-angled shot. With his bayonet he quickly cut some turfs from the ground and piled them up into a firm and solid gun-rest, then aimed above the head of his victim. He breathed a few times slowly and regularly. After a last deep breath he took the trigger, held his breath and pulled. The whipping bang destroyed the silence. Bringing his weapon instantly back into position after its momentary recoil he had his target back in his telescopic sight in a fraction of a second and saw the bullet strike above the navel of the unsuspecting Russian. He doubled up like a jack-knife. His cry of pain and the panicked voices of his comrades blew across to Sepp. The fatally injured man rolled over on his side and a huge pool of blood from his back was apparent in the sand. The other Russians scattered in all directions like chickens startled by a hawk and nobody dared to help their dying comrade. After a few minutes his sufferings seemed to have ended because his movements ceased. Meanwhile Sepp saw a rush of activity among uniformed Russians above the riverbank, and moments later he heard the sound of a descending mortar shell that detonated on the shore below him. It was time to get away before things became serious. He wriggled away like a weasel and ran back to the riflemen's trenches, protected by the hill, while shells destroyed the firing position behind him.

The host of the coffee break welcomed him back with a certain spitefulness in his voice. He had heard the single gunshot break the silence of the afternoon and immediately knew what had happened. 'Shit, was that necessary? Our cosiness has had it. Boys, get into your clothes, Ivan will be giving us hell. Mister Artful Shooter here couldn't wait to destroy our idyll.' He had hardly finished speaking when the first salvos of machine-gun fire raked their position, followed by a short mortar strike that landed behind the trenches without doing any damage. Sepp used the sudden activity to slip away gracefully and not expose himself to any further invective.

The next day single dangerously precise shots began hitting II Battalion's positions, a clear indication that a specialist on the Russian side was taking on the problem of Sepp Allerberger. But Sepp stayed quite calm, because a duel across the river was not possible. Of course, he did start to double his attention.

It was amazing how quickly soldiers settled into a position and made it cosy. Their few weeks in that place resulted in encampments like self-contained villages. As if out of nowhere, they created every possible sort of utility. They built laundries and barbers' salons and showers. They cooked and fried and organized meals. There were even chickens around, which were guarded with their keepers' lives as a tasty source of roast meals and eggs. But the soldiers were worse than hungry foxes, and successful chicken thieves were held in great esteem by their comrades.

Sepp and the battalion runners with whom he worked had no such opportunities to cultivate a camp life. They were therefore dependent on ruthless theft in order to get a varied and mixed diet, and realizing this their comrades watched them carefully. But it was just a question of days before they set to work.

Because Sepp could freely move about the battalion area he was the one to track down potential victims. The sergeant of the neighbouring company had a real humdinger of a chicken, lovingly called Josephine, which supplied him with an egg a day because he took such good care of it. This he ate himself or traded for other delicacies. A single chicken was an ideal target, because if Sepp acted skilfully there was no danger of being betrayed by the screams of other birds. Being a specialist and marksman, Sepp was unanimously chosen as the assassin: 'Sepp, this is clearly a job for a marksman! Your hunting instincts and your catlike smoothness make you the obvious choice.'

It was a new moon and the sky was cloudy, ideal conditions for a commando operation of this delicate kind. While his comrades made a fire and readied everything for swift and smooth preparation of their meal, Sepp put on full camouflage for the first and last time. He blackened his face and hands with charcoal and tied branches onto his hat and uniform. Lightly rustling in the wind, he disappeared into the darkness, although not without first asking a comrade who'd been a farmer about the quickest way of liquidating a chicken with one's bare hands.

Like a panther he crept carefully and silently to the dugouts of the neighbouring company. The chicken was dozing unsuspectingly in its usual hiding place, lovingly made out of wicker baskets intended for artillery ammunition. The guard was standing about 20m away sharing a cigarette with a comrade, which they smoked behind a helmet in order not to reveal themselves by the glow. Sepp's nerves tightened. He knew that he'd suffer if he was caught. Now he was at the wicker basket. He hardly dared to breathe and his pounding heart was almost bursting as he raised the lid of the basket millimetre by millimetre. There was the chicken, with its head under its wing in deep sleep. Now was not the time for mistakes. He leant the basket lid against his forehead to have both hands free. His hands approached the chicken. Only a few centimetres left, and then he had a grip on its neck with his left hand. At the same moment he managed to take the chicken's rising head in his right hand, and before it knew what was happening a short energetic twist of his hands ended Josephine's life with a silent crack. Sepp remained still for a moment to observe the guard, but he just continued whispering to his comrade and clearly hadn't noticed anything. Quickly Sepp stowed the chicken away inside his camouflage jacket and disappeared as silently as he had come.

A quarter of an hour later the chicken was plucked and drawn, and all traces of its demise were buried far away. After another hour and it was braised and divided up on to four mess tins, a banquet for Sepp and his comrades. To mark the occasion they washed it down with a bottle of schnapps. Full and drunk they fell into a well-deserved and restful sleep – from which they were torn by the screams of the bereaved sergeant the next morning. 'What dirty pig has stolen my chicken? It can only be one of your company, the tracks of the assassin are leading in your direction. Not one of my men would have dared to touch Josephine – I'd have shot him personally.' Sepp and his comrades struggled to look surprised and shocked and obviously succeeded, because they got away with it, even though the sergeant showed that he clearly suspected them. He had no proof but he promised to keep at it, and if he should find any, he threatened, he'd have them court-martialled and shot as looters.

Between 25–28 May the battalion's tranquility was ended, but only for a short while. The survivors of GJR 138 returned and 3 Gebirgsjäger Division was transferred to the Aurel Pass in the Carpathian Mountains. Their positions followed the course of the Moldau, which was now between them and the Russian front. Besides this watery obstacle the forested approaches of the slowly rising mountains were good cover for the riflemen. The terrain lying before them on the other side of the river was very open, flat and highly visible. Fate was good to the division, for the Russian focus of attack was transferred to a place north of their positions, and they had only light skirmishes with the enemy.

Along with really beautiful weather this unexpected rest and peace provided the exhausted riflemen with an opportunity to recuperate. Quickly their camp life was re-established. Homely bunkers were created and everything was organized to make life as pleasant as possible.

The Landsers were electrified when the latrine patrol told them that a Wehrmacht brothel was about to be transferred to their quiet sector for two weeks, for edification and for psychosexual reasons. War reduced a soldier's life to the absolutely essential things: survival, scoffing, guzzling, and – if possible – fucking. The last, of course, was only possible – other than by rape, which was not to everybody's taste and was often punished – if troops were in a relatively peaceful situation and could fraternize with the native population, or if there was a brothel in the neighbourhood. When a unit was able to relax the strain of constant fighting often unloaded itself in the form of an overpowering sexual drive. Relief from this urge assumed very high importance, simply in order to maintain discipline. While officers and sergeants helped themselves to female Marketendienerinnen – Wehrmacht helpers, called 'Officers' mattresses' in Landser slang – the lowly military rank of a Landser meant he did not have accesss to such women. For him there was just rape or the brothel.

When the opportunity presented itself the latter establishments were stormed by the sex-starved soldiers. But their visits presented one little problem: they were observed by medical personnel and ended with disinfection in order to prevent venereal disease. More than a few soldiers deliberately infected themselves with these diseases so as to get away from the front. In order to treat them special hospitals were eventually established, called 'knights' castles' among the Landsers, where their syphilis was dealt with using sometimes very rough methods of treatment. Usually a stay in a knights' castle was enough to encourage the exercise of sexual discipline in the future. Experts on the subject still remember the *Dittelstab* with little rapture. This was a kind of round file used to open encrusted focuses of disease inside the urethra to be disinfected later. This was done without anaesthetic, of course. Moreover, repeatedly infected soldiers were subjected to disciplinary punishment as early as the first years of the war on the grounds of their disease being a form of self-mutilation.

The strict disinfection of brothel visitors' urethras theoretically prevented problems. Landsers experienced with what might be termed 'commercial favours' knew the details of this procedure and had great fun regaling younger comrades with their incisive experiences. But in the innocence of his years Sepp foresaw none of it.

During this period of rest Sepp met his marksman comrade Josef Roth again. They exchanged ideas, drank and talked about sex. Being young neither of them had much experience of the opposite sex, but faced with the immediate temptation of the brothel they discussed the pros and cons of visiting it to find out what they had been missing. After all, it might be the last chance they had for such things. Finally they came to a conclusion: now or never, before it was too late. Josef likened the delicate matter to a question of fate. 'Think of it, perhaps it's your last opportunity to put one away. Maybe tomorrow you catch one and die without having fucked. A terrible fate!'

While they were talking Sepp's eyes fell on a sergeant-major from the detachment that had just brought up ammunition, who was sitting on the running board of an Opel Blitz waiting for a load to take back. It was the Viking with the red moustache! He caught Sepp's look and had obviously heard their talk. 'Hey, you horny bastards, you get a hard on thinking of firm butts. Ha ha!' Regaining his composure and seeing their surprised faces he added: 'Honestly boys, let it be and profit from the life experiences of an old sergeant. The five minutes of fun don't make up for the pain afterwards.' There was a meaningful silence after that, interrupted by Roth, now a bit drunk, saying: 'Perhaps, you clever dick, you'll tell us your great secret!' 'Well,' the Viking continued, 'as a future academic I'll let you profit from my experience. And if you're good and listen to uncle, you can spare yourself a lot of trouble.' 'Now don't make such a melodrama of it, fire away,' griped Roth. 'Okay, a bit of cynicism has to be allowed,' the sergeant relented. 'First give me a swig of your gut-rot.' After swallowing deeply he started his story with a satisfied sigh.

'Well, it was a while ago now. When I had to go to the corps depot one time my co-driver was a sergeant, a real cunning old devil I'll tell you. For the whole ride he just talked about sex and food. He was totally showing off – what he had fingered and where he had screwed. Once we arrived at the depot he, of course, knew where you could get it. What can I say? He dragged me along to the next brothel. I didn't want to look like I was scared. First we drank and then we stuck in. The brothel was in a former school. We'd hardly opened the door when a medical sergeant grabbed us by the scruffs of our necks. I tell you, he was a great hulking brute. Immediately he yelled at us: "Where's your condom?" Surprised, I looked at him. He grinned back and rummaged in his pocket. "The condom, you housewives. No one fights with a blank weapon here," he added. I hadn't thought of that. But for the trivial sum of 30 *pfennig* I could have a Wehrmacht

condom. "Fucking twice without any extras, that'
fuck." Catching my uncomprehending look he
Reichsmarks, you ferrets." I'd been there a minut
disillusioned. But a real mountain rifleman never
of adverse circumstances. I paid the medic and h
paper bag with the condom.

'Then he said: "The chickens are over there in the classroom," and with these words he pushed us into the next room. Before us five lightly dressed Romanian women lounged on worn out upholstery, looking bored as we timidly entered. Quickly my comrade grabbed a madam and disappeared behind a curtain with her, and probably he was already at work while I stood there like water in a curve. My erotic desires were there in front of me and I couldn't even move. Now it had got serious I would have left if I could. I stood there paralyzed, my face reddening. Meanwhile the women were talking among themselves, deciding who should take care of this stripling. Finally one of them got up, took my hand without any further comment and led me behind another curtain. Very excited, I didn't notice the plainness of this love nest as my companion opened my trousers and they dropped to my ankles.

'It was like being struck by electricity when she took it with a firm but tender grip. I have to decorate the following to torment you virgins a bit.' With a theatrical gesture the Viking assumed a conspiratorial expression, and Sepp and Roth hung on every word of his detailed description of what followed. 'Attention children,' he continued. 'The little girl who made a pass at me was looking really delicious and she knew her business. "Shh, trrrust me," she cooed, grabbing my loins, and then she started to caress me rhythmically with both hands. Shudders of lust took me. I pulled her face towards me and covered it with kisses. She let me do it, knowing my youth and naivety.

'Greedily I sucked in the smell of her body and her hair, my hands losing themselves in the silky shimmering black hair that flowed over her shoulders like silk. Greedily my hands followed the shape of her body. The fear, strain and desire of the last few months – of my entire life – were concentrated in this one moment. Her breath tickled my ears almost unbearably. Tenderly her tongue followed the shape of my neck, nibblingly caressed my earlobe, and whooshed lightly across my throat, touching my cheeks, and inspired by my desire her hands an to move faster. Shuddering in pleasure, I sank onto the mattress n the floor and gave myself over to the ecstasy of the moment.

'Supposedly tender embraces give you a misleading feeling of security in the cold of these troubled times. Letting you fall, but being caught in the moment. Like a beetle her tongue tickled across my stomach, circling my navel, sweeping across my shame and clasping my holy of holies. The happiness of the moment sent shivers of excitement and warmth. The cruelty of war faded for a few minutes.

'My body wound round and cuddled up to the strange but familiar moment. My grasping hands and her firm but tender fingers found each other, to embrace and hold for that brief instant. My tenderness sought in her face for a moment of fulfilment, but I found myself looking into eyes filled with inscrutable and empty sadness. They cut me off and sent me on a voyage of lonely introspection. Fate or destiny? Happiness and pain are the iron elements of fate. Greedily I devoured the fleeting moment of happiness, until pain determined reality again.'

Sepp and Roth sat there with mouths agape, speechless at this almost lyrical interlude. 'Man, are you some kind of poet or what?' Roth grumbled. 'Can't you just tell us what happened?' 'Oh, the gentlemen want it a bit simpler, for proles,' said the Viking, his poetic flow disrupted. 'So, if you want to make notes: the girl gave me such a head that my balls were almost bursting. Do you understand now?' 'All right, old man,' Sepp calmed him down. 'I'm enjoying the story. Go on, we'll shut up.' With that he elbowed Roth in the ribs.

'Okay,' said the Viking, and he started again. 'With glazed eyes, relieved, and with a new self-image of myself as a man, I emerged from the shabby cubicle. I bounced light-footedly towards the exit, only to be torn back to reality by the strident voice of the ambulance sergeant. "Not so fast! First come here and down your pants." At first I again failed to understand what was required because of the medic's northern slang (he came from Münster in Westphalia). "Just to clean your dick isn't enough," he said more intelligibly, "we gotta try the Chemical Mace. So don't be shy, show your noodle." He had already pulled me over and grabbed my holiest with the routine of a butcher. Quick as lightning he pushed a syringe without a needle into my urethra and injected about a hundred millilitres of a green liquid into me. Burning fiery hot it shot into my belly as the disinfectant solution cleared a path into my bladder. Grinding my teeth and with my fists clenched so tightly that my knuckles went white, I endured my martyrdom, unable to defend myself because the medic's iron grip tolerated no contradiction. "That hurts, eh?" said this representative of military health care, enjoying my painful desperation. The sensual pleasure of the previous half hour was swept away. "Put your noodle away," the medic bawled at me. "In five minutes you may piss, but not a second earlier." My sergeant, the old bastard, had the total routine down pat. He took it like it was nothing. I can still see the fat, gloating grin on his face while he watched me doubled up in pain. Observed by a severe sanitary lance-corporal, I hopped back and forth in front of the former schoolboys' toilet, my little sausage pinched between thumb and forefinger. I suspect that the vindictive sanitary guy stretched the time out, seeing my pain, until the words "Now you may!" released me. With ecstatic rapture I gave the sulphonamide solution its well-earned freedom. The feeling of relief was almost orgasmic and nearly better than the joy of my sexual fulfilment. In the meantime my sergeant couldn't hold back his laughter.

'After a last inspection of my genitals I was finally allowed to leave that hospitable place. I staggered back to freedom and swore never again to have sex under such circumstances.'

After this dramatic description the two sexually motivated aspirants felt a violent burning in their pants just from listening. 'I usually prefer to learn from my own experience,' Roth commented, 'but in this case I'll listen to the good uncle. Sepp, our action is postponed.' Sepp was quite happy about that, because he hadn't been too enthusiastic even before the Viking told his tale. He resisted all temptation of this kind until they returned to their homeland.

Meanwhile it seemed that miracles still occurred occasionally. The division was re-equipped unexpectedly back to its full wartime strength of men and material. The officers knew this would be the last time, though, because among them it was already acknowledged that the war was lost. They were motivated by just one thought: to deter the Russians from taking revenge on their homeland. The Russians were gathering for a new strike against the few German and Romanian units before them. The lull before the oncoming storm would be the final chance for the division's few remaining 'old hands' who had survived the murderous battles more or less unhurt to see their families one last time. As far as possible they were given leave. Sepp, even after just one year with the division, counted among those who had survived a long time, but at only 19½ years of age he had to give way to fathers and men who had served for even longer. In addition the few experienced marksmen were indispensable. Sepp's chances of a holiday were nil. But his battalion commander Captain Kloss, who liked him very much, knew a little trick that would get him home.

Chapter 11

'Mistakes are made just once'

In the last quarter of 1943 the Wehrmacht started to install sniper schools in its largest training camps. Here, in courses lasting just four weeks, they tried to prepare chosen soldiers for the special role of marksmen. The soldiers chosen for these courses were a mixture of freshly called-up recruits and old hands with extensive front line experience who'd been selected by their officers as potential marksmen. All of them would get – besides a marksman's gun – the necessary special training they required. The marksman training for the Gebirgsjäger took place in Austria, in the military training area called 'Seetaleralpe' near the city of Judenburg. From here it was not far to Sepp's home village. So Captain Kloss slyly 'demoted' him to the rank of an occasional marksman who needed to attend a special course at Seetaleralpe. Since this almost took him home, he could afterwards take his ten-day home leave from there. So on 30 May 1944 Sepp and ten other men given leave left their comrades in the back of an Opel Blitz and set off along the division's supply line. Before leaving he handed his Russian marksman's rifle to the regimental Armourer, who gave it to another rifleman while Sepp was present. 'Do you see the notches in the stock?' the NCO asked the recipient. 'Every notch is one Russian less. To take over this gun is an honour and an obligation. Do your best, and show Sepp when he returns that you've represented him worthily.' The young Landser looked quite amazed and embarrassed by these heroic words, but Sepp put his hand on his shoulder saying: 'Don't let them make you crazy. Just be careful and don't get your arse hurt.' He reached into his pocket and brought out a handful of Russian explosive bullets wrapped in his handkerchief, which he kept for use in special circumstances, and handed them to his comrade. 'I don't need them now. If you need a real bang in the gun, and want to be sure of something spectacular in your sights, use one of these. It's explosive ammunition. But be economical with it, it's very rare. Other than that, just stay safe – you have to tell me what happened when I get back in six weeks.'

The lorry's motor howled, Sepp jumped into the back and shook his comrade's hand again. With it an indefinable premonition of death hit him, and suddenly he thought: 'Poor dog, he'll be caught quickly.' 'Are you girls through with your heartbreaking goodbye? I'll start crying soon,' yelled the lorry driver. Then he stepped on the accelerator and in a cloud of dust and exhaust Sepp's comrades were left behind. Sepp wondered if he would see them again. A strange mixture of relief at being able to escape the hell of war for a while, and guilt at leaving his comrades behind, took hold of him. After just a year in the army his former life had been wiped away and the daily fight for survival had become his only reality. And he seemed to be addicted to the brutal fascination of killing or being killed. But before long such profound thoughts were washed away by the sonorous humming of the lorry's motor. Cosy sleepiness came over him.

It was two days before he realized that he had got away from the war. The tranquil, undisturbed landscape through which he travelled by train seemed almost unreal. Whereas his journey to the front had taken more than ten days a year ago it now took only five to get to his destination, Judenburg. Sepp was lucky, because a lance corporal who had delivered a parcel to the station for his company chief took him back to the training area in his jeep. Sepp looked forward to the training with mixed emotions, because he vividly remembered his basic training, in which the instructors were always yelling and the soldiers were trained in stupid drill. He had only agreed to being delegated to attend the course because he didn't want to miss the opportunity of a few weeks of good meals, regular sleep and the chance of a few days at home.

He was amazed when he was welcomed in almost amiable fashion when he reported in at the sergeant's office at the training school. No standing to attention, just a friendly and pleasant introduction to his quarters and the approaching course. It became obvious that here it was all about the qualified training of specialists, not the drill-like hammering in of basic knowledge.

Within the extensive training area the marksmen's school was in a separate hut complex. Sepp shared his room with four 18-year-olds from the Mittenwalderland, who had been sent straight to the school after their three months' basic training. They had proved themselves to be extraordinarily good shots with stoic attitudes and very good powers of observation. When he entered the room his eyes fell on a framed text on the wall. There was written in Gothic letters:

'The marksman is the hunter among soldiers! His duty is heavy and demands the whole man, physically and mentally. Only a completely convinced and steadfast soldier can become a marksman. It is only possible to defeat the enemy if you have learned to hate and pursue him with the whole strength of your soul! Being a marksman is a decoration for the soldier! He fights unseen. His strength lies in Red Indian-like use of terrain combined with perfect camouflage, catlike agility and masterly control of his weapon. Awareness of his skills gives him safety and superiority and guarantees his victory.'

These heroic words did not leave him unmoved; a certain pride welled up within him. But at the same time this was tempered by his awareness of the reality of war and its mercilessness. And something inside him froze at that, and he thought: 'If you knew what war is really like, if you were dying, sayings like these would be of no use to you.'

His training course started the same day, a Monday, with a lesson in special weapons dedicated to the topic of guns with telescopic sights. The instructor was a sergeant with an artificial leg. It came out that almost all the trainers were experienced front-line soldiers disabled by wounds. Many were even former marksmen, who, like Sepp, had worked hard to learn their skills until they were no longer fit for duty at the front. The course consisted of sixty soldiers organized in groups of five. Each group had its own teacher for every topic.

On a table were four guns with telescopic sights. There were three K98k models and a weapon none of them had seen before. At the front Sepp had heard rumours about a new self-loading rifle, but he hadn't seen one in his unit. It was a Walther Model 43 with a Voigtländer Model 4 telescopic sight. Beside it was a K98k with a really tiny telescopic sight of about 15cm length named the Model 41. Another of the K98s lying before them had a 6x magnification Dialytan telescopic sight, produced by the Hensoldt company, on a massive swivel mounting called a 'Mauser mounting' by the trainer but in modern terminology called a tower-swivel mounting. This was considered the best and most solid telescopic-sight mounting for the K98k.

After a few remarks concerning the efficiency of the single

telescopic sights and mountings he elaborated on the carbine with the swivel mounting, because it was the weapon all the course's participants would be equipped with. In the afternoon they went on the shooting range to try all four of these weapons. Sepp took great interest in the range and the brightness and brilliance of the Zeiss and Hensoldt sight, which was clearly better than his former Russian weapon. But very similar to this was the sight of the self-loading rifle. Shooting with the Walther was very easy because part of the recoil was absorbed by the automatic reloading mechanism, but its precision lagged behind the K98 carbines. The weapon with the little ZF 41 sight amused everyone. It shot quite well, but you could hardly see anything through the tiny sight. The trainer's comment was: 'Such shit can only be created by those idiots in administration. Those armchair farters know as much about marksmen as a cow knows about singing songs.'

After this they had to perform various exercises shooting with the normal K98k over open sights, standing, kneeling, lying and at different distances from 50m to 300m. They had no lack of ammunition and were able to go through their exercises without having to endure the usual drill that applied in firing ranges. Training and learning were clearly the priority.

The next day they went out into the grounds of the training area to estimate distances and to assess the tactical prospects of different types of hiding place. The afternoon was spent on the range again, and this proved to be the case every day during the course. Later in the week the subjects of camouflage and special positions were added to the curriculum. Sepp didn't learn much new from these. Some of the camouflages and positions seemed pretty time-consuming and unrealistic to him, because the daily routine of war didn't leave sufficient time or means to achieve them. For example, there were hollowed-out trees, a full body camouflage made out of tree bark and an earth seat under a milestone rebuilt from plywood. But in his own experience camouflage had to be quick, effective and easy to create from the simplest materials available, and should limit the marksman's mobility as little as possible. The course leader knew Sepp had served as a marksman but was unaware of his experience and skills. As the course went on, however, he recognized his expertise.

The timetable for the last day of their first week showed a class was to be held in the 'shooting garden'. Sepp and his comrades had no idea what this meant and were curious about it. Great was their amazement when they found themselves led to a miniature landscape. About 50m in front of their firing butts was a model of an idyllic valley containing a village and roads, all built to a reduced scale. It made them feel like Gulliver in Lilliput. They were issued with special weapons for this training, because they had to shoot with small-calibre sporting guns. The weapons were made by Gustloff and Walther and were equipped with telescopic sights. The Gustloff rifle had a Model 41 sight on the left side, while the Walther gun had a 4x magnification telescope by the Oigee company of Berlin.

Their task was to observe the model landscape and shoot at little figures as soon as they appeared somewhere, in windows, behind houses or among the trees. There were even vehicles and horse carriages that moved along the roads, and they had to shoot at them too. Sepp's tactical experience showed especially well in this training. His experienced eye picked out the slightest movement and it was seldom more than thirty seconds before his shot hit its target, but only with the 4x telescopic sight on the Walther. The Model 41 sight had such a small diameter and limited range of vision that almost all the students considered it entirely unsuitable for use by marksmen. The talents of a perfectionist like Sepp shone in this practice, and were so rare among the usual participants of such courses that their instructor foresaw he could do little to improve his skills.

Regular practice in the shooting garden was part of the training programme throughout the course. Not only did they have to shoot into the model village, but also into constantly revised and rebuilt landscapes, in which unknown targets were hidden that they had to find and fight.

An ongoing competition between the candidates started with their first day in the shooting garden, because the results of the daily practices were recorded on separate pages of the course logbook. The best student on the course would be discovered this way and would be rewarded with a big parcel of luxuries including spirits, cigarettes, chocolate, and canned meat.

All participants of the course had to keep a little notebook and carry it with them. In this they wrote down such things as observations regarding the terrain and their shooting scores. This was to accustom the future marksmen to keeping a similar notebook when they returned to the front, in which they should enter details about the terrain, changes of firing position and hits scored. Sepp tipped off his comrades to always encode all entries that might betray their function as marksmen, and never to enter their name. It would be even better if they entered no hits into the book at all, he said, but kept them in a separate nameless list held by their sergeant. Such discretion would probably save their lives if they were captured, since their role would remain unknown. Captured marksmen on the Eastern Front were always tortured and killed. The young men paled at Sepp's warning.

Monday of the second week was a big day for the course participants, because a lorry arrived with big boxes stencilled with the Mauser company code, 'byf'. Everybody helped to unload them and they were able to satisfy their curiosity by opening one. Inside was a brand new K98k carbine with a big 4x magnification sight in a tower-swivel mounting. During the next few hours every student received one of these. The number was entered into his book with the remark 'telescopic sight rifle'. This meant that each particular weapon was only to be used by its recipient. They were told that they would not really own their weapons until they had successfully completed the course. This increased their determination to pass the course, especially among the younger soldiers without any fighting experience. Sepp got a carbine with a sight by the Hensoldt company, which had the codename 'bmj'. It was much shorter than the Russian rifle he had left behind and the sight was much better, as he had already found during the demonstration of the various guns the previous week. Proud of their new weapons, they could hardly wait to get on the firing range again to try them out. After his very first shot Sepp knew that he had a super weapon in his hands.

Now, for the first time, they also received special ammunition for marksmen. The instructor explained that these were cartridges with an especially precise load, such as were usually used during gun making and repairing in order to determine the accuracy of a weapon. He recommended that they should beg their battalion Armourer to issue them with such ammunition as often as possible after their return to the front line. After this they enthusiastically set about calibrating their weapons. The basic calibration was made over a distance of a hundred metres. To do this they removed the breech and then, resting the weapon on sandbags, aimed the barrel of the gun at the centre of the target by looking directly through it. By alternating between looking through the barrel and the sight, the sight's reticle was brought into alignment with the barrel. The sideways deviation was then corrected by the alternate loosening and tightening of two screws on the back foot of the mounting by means of a special key that was included with every weapon. After this basic adjustment, the fine tuning was made during the practice shoot.

The day ended with them being instructed never to let their weapon out of their hands. During the rest of the course they carried it with them the whole day. In every bedroom there was a gun rack in which the weapons were only put overnight. In this way they learned how to take care of their carbines and keep them from damage, especially the optics. Every fall or hard knock to the sight could ruin the adjustment and seriously affect its accuracy. Sepp, of course, had become wise to this by bitter experience, during his early days with his Russian telescopic rifle, and handling his weapon carefully had now become second nature. But the other participants of the course had trouble with handling their carbines for the first few days. But they learnt, since apart from the fact that the sights had to be re-adjusted after every fall or knock, there were gymnastic interludes for the clumsy directly after each such incident – twenty push-ups and thirty knee-bends with the carbine held out before them.

Their visit to the shooting garden the next day was described as 'choice and improvement of positions'. But before they went to practise they were shown a marksmen training film in the classroom. To their amazement the film was Russian with German subtitles. It was shot in 1935 and gave an impressive insight into the high standard of Russian training. Before screening it, their trainer commented: 'Just take a close look at this. Ivan isn't bad. His marksmen were making trouble for us already during the advance of 1941–42 and we were standing there in short shirts. Then we didn't even know how to spell "marksman". Losses among our officers were disastrous. If there were no heavy weapons, the Russian marksmen stopped us for days. With telescopic rifles captured from Ivan we tried to do something about that. But the swine were really good and we had to learn the hard way. Finally I too found my match. You can see where he hit me. I was damn lucky to escape death once again.' With that he lowered his head so that they could all see the massive scar from which a glass eye stared fixedly from where his left eye had been. 'It was a twist of fate and great publicity for the Zeiss company that the Ivan's bullet bounced off my binoculars and I just lost an eye, and not my life,' he went on. As already said, almost all the trainers at the school were former marksmen who were no longer fit for fighting because of serious injuries, but could do a valuable job by transmitting their experience and knowledge to the recruits. 'So be aware that the enemy has professionals too. And I can give you one hot tip – piss off as soon as you recognize a hostile marksman is after you. When there is, there's just one thing you can do: change position after every shot.'

With a monotonous rattle the movie went through the projector. His comrades watched the show with dutiful attention, but Sepp did not see anything new and had to fight against sleep after a few minutes in the darkened room. Like a rabbit he dozed with open eyes in a half comatose state that only experienced soldiers can control in classrooms, before a scene in the film suddenly caught his attention. It showed a Russian marksman company preparing positions in the treetops at the edge of a forest. The subtitle read: 'Leafy treetops are an excellent position. The shooter is not seen, but he has a wide view of the landscape and an outstanding field of fire!'

Shit, Sepp thought, and immediately he put his hand up. The lessons were very inter-active, and immediately accommodated questions, suggestions and answers. His request to speak was noticed at once and the film was stopped. Sepp said that he could tell them more about the scene that had just been shown from his own experience, and he told them all about his fight with the female marksmen in the trees. The awkward silence that followed was broken by their trainer with the remark: 'Listen to that, boys! This rifleman knows what he's talking about, because he's survived more than a year as a marksman at the front. And you should hammer it into your brain that mistakes are made just once by a marksman, and in ninety per cent of cases you're done for at that. So take in all the useful hints you can get. Every good piece of advice you can get and keep might save your arse one day.'

The days passed, and Sepp enjoyed eating well and sleeping regularly. On the one hand he was happy to escape the daily fear for his life for a while, but on the other hand he often thought of his comrades and how they might be getting along. He tried to find out what 3 Gebirgsjäger Division was doing, but the heavily censored newspapers didn't say anything worthwhile. On a few occasions the trainers were able to pass on information that soldiers on leave had given them. According to this it was relatively quiet in 3 GD's sector.

Theory and practical instruction complemented each other. Over the next days they were put into hypothetical combat situations in which they had to act independently, and the demands placed on them were constantly increased, climaxing in a very realistic scenario. The day before this, everybody had to prepare a marksman's position under given circumstances, and they had to move into this the next morning. Shortly before moving into their positions they were given a description of the prevailing combat situation, which was that two enemy marksmen were out to get them. Two instructors would observe and record every opportunity they gave the enemy snipers to hit them: any visible movement by the students would mean they were dead. Then they were told that they wouldn't be allowed to leave their positions until dawn the next day. A look of horror spread across the other students' faces. Sepp knew why. Being tied to one spot for so long presents a number of logistical problems: eating, drinking, pissing, and shitting – when, how and where were they to be done? Sepp, as a veteran, had chosen and prepared his position accordingly, so that these things could be achieved as far as possible. His inexperienced comrades faced a more challenging ordeal. After that they tagged a light camouflage of grass and fresh branches onto their helmets and moved into their positions.

An oppressively hot day was coming up. In the shimmering sunlight the training area stretched away before them. By about noon the sweat was flowing from them like water, their limbs were starting to hurt, and various physical needs were demanding their attention. For the first few hours Sepp just observed the approaches and recorded significant things. During this time he managed to make out the instructors' positions. With that, all the important tasks of the day were done as far as he was concerned. As usual he had prepared his position in a way that would enable him to disappear unseen. This not only provided better security against enemy grenades but also allowed him to endure the long wait in relative comfort. He had already dug an additional hole into which he could pee by turning slightly to one side, and he always did his 'big jobs' before he started his day. Finally, as an experienced marksman he always made sure that he had water and food with him, even if it was only a crust or some biscuits. So he just slid back into the protecting depth of his position and spent his day dozing, dreaming and chewing. After daybreak next day the order came to withdraw and they gathered for the march back to camp. Many of his inexperienced comrades were dragging themselves along utterly exhausted. They all had a big piss spot on their pants and many were walking with legs apart and faces distorted by disgust, having shitted in their pants. One of their instructors couldn't resist a complacent grin when he saw this. 'Boys, I have a hot tip for you: always shit in the morning. Anyone who leaves home without shitting only has himself to blame.' 'The arses did that on purpose,' hissed Sepp's neighbour.

The next day the positions of every single candidate were visited and judged according to their suitability. Sepp was asked to explain the pros and cons of his own, and he willingly gave his comrades the benefit of his experience at the front, explaining that the essence of selecting a good position involved the big three big 'hows': how to get into the position unseen; how to get out of the position unseen; and how to reach the next position quickly and unseen.

The rest of the course seemed to fly by, and many of the participants started to feel uneasy at the prospect of their approaching deployment to the front. They got a foretaste during a training day about ammunition.

Marksmen often moved about ahead of their own lines. If spotted by the enemy they were usually subjected to the fire of heavy infantry weapons. It was therefore an advantage to recognize these weapons by their sound in order to take the right defensive action. If he was shot at by a mortar, for example, it was just a question of time until the enemy either got his range or peppered the area until they finally hit the marksman. Under these circumstances it was necessary for him to leave his position as fast as possible, and unable to make a covered withdrawal all he could do was bravely jump up and zigzag back to his own lines at the run. As already explained, among marksmen this was called the 'rabbit jump'. It called for a high degree of willpower, but it was the only way to survive in such a situation. The 'rabbit jump' was consequently practised repeatedly during the course, though many marksmen would later die because when the moment of truth came they stayed in their holes paralyzed by panic and fear.

While the mortar could be demonstrated to them by live shots, the sound of one of the most feared Russian weapons of all was only available as a gramophone record. Known as the 'Stalin organ' by front-line soldiers, this was a lorry-borne multiple rocket launcher that could turn an area the size of a soccer field into an inferno of buzzing splinters and churned up earth in just one strike. The recording of its rhythmic howling sound turned up to full volume made them shudder. It brought back vivid memories to Sepp, who could almost taste the sulphur, smoke and blood on his tongue. Asked by his comrades how they could protect themselves against such a weapon, he had just a short answer, while a shadow came over his face that made him look ten years older: 'Only a deep hole will help you.

Then press your arse-cheeks together and pray.'

The session concluded with the introduction of ammunition that was new to infantry use, the so-called B-cartridge. This had originally been developed as a tracer round for the machine guns of fighter planes, the 'B' standing for *Beobachtung* (observation). These cartridges exploded when they struck and thus indicated the accuracy of the fire. The fire of the aircraft could then be swiftly adjusted. This ammunition was very expensive to produce and was consequently reserved for its original purpose for a long time. But the Russians, who had this kind of ammunition even before the beginning of the campaign, had already started using it against infantry. The brutal effect of such projectiles was understandably feared among the Landsers, in particular because Russian marksmen liked to use it. Sepp, of course, already knew about such cartridges, having used captured Russian rounds. He therefore considered it appropriate that such ammunition should be available to the Germans as well. According to the Geneva Convention explosive ammunition for hand weapons was actually illegal, but the situation on the Eastern Front had now slipped so far that the end justified any and all means available. In a short shooting demonstration saplings about 5cm in diameter were cut down effortlessly with this ammunition.

From the fourth week of the course the training became even more realistic. Besides daily basic practices on the firing range and in the garden, the future marksmen underwent practical lessons on how to change positions. For these, combat situations were imitated as realistically as possible. These lessons included moving undiscovered between other units practising military exercises in the training area, and hunting for each other as marksmen would have to in the field. Finally their shooting practise in the 'garden' was integrated into these lessons, and they had not only to find the hidden targets, but also to fire at them with live ammunition. This involved locating and shooting at dummies within a set time. If they didn't succeed they received negative marks from the instructors, and the dire warning that they would be dead under real front-line conditions. In this way Sepp's inexperienced comrades got a better idea of the danger that they would face in the field. When these practical lessons began the trainee marksmen 'died' like flies. Even Sepp made mistakes, though this was because the training adhered to official Wehrmacht policy that a marksman's battlefield role was strictly offensive, whereas Sepp would have resolved many situations with greater caution. A good marksman had to know when to disappear, but the course made no allowance for individuals taking such decisions.

The course had flown by and it ended with a celebration on the last Saturday evening. Their sergeant managed to get hold of a barrel of beer, a few bottles of spirits, and some sides of pork, so they made the most of the very welcome summer weather by organizing a barbecue. Tables and chairs were brought from their barracks. They constructed a grill out of a cleaned-up gate, wire, and a pine wood trestle. The glowing fire made the air smell spicy. But before they settled down to enjoy the evening, the sergeant made them all line up. On a table in front of him were fifty-six marksmen's rifles and a pile of books. The candidates were called up individually. The four trainees who did not pass the course were called up first: these would return to their units as ordinary riflemen. Then the graduating marksmen were called up in reverse order, lowest scores first. With a handshake the sergeant handed each of them in turn the rifle they had used on the course, their service record book, and a pretty paper from the orderly room inscribed with the ten commandments of a marksman.

As everybody had expected, Sepp was one of the three best on the course, who were called up last. While the sergeant's congratulations were water off a duck's back, Sepp's prize of an ammunition box filled with food was very welcome, since it meant he would not have to visit his family empty-handed.

With the handing-over of their rifles the trainees had officially become marksmen. But whereas the more inexperienced soldiers were happy about their new status as elite fighters, front-line veterans like Sepp regarded the future with anxiety and foreboding – but not for too long: the life of a Landser belonged to the moment, and right now there was food and beer to be enjoyed. So he got stuck in and grabbed what he could, because he knew that each day could be his last.

While the majority of the course participants were sitting on trains heading for the east, on Sunday afternoon Sepp got a lift to Mittenwald aboard a lorry and walked to his home village from there. He had forewarned his family of his visit by letter and his parents and sisters were waiting for him when he knocked on the door. There was no need for words. His parents embraced him emotionally while his sisters stood by uncertainly. Then Sepp turned to them and said: 'Look what I've got for you, girls.' And with that he unslung his rifle and, leaning it against the wall, took off his backpack and pulled out bars of chocolate in red tinfoil from among the titbits he'd won.

Chapter 12

'Something's up with the Romanians'

As far as his family knew Sepp had been on some sort of adventure holiday for the last few months if the omnipresent propaganda machine was to be believed. 'Tell us, how is the war?' they asked. 'Boy, you look bad,' his mother exclaimed. 'Don't they give you enough to eat in the army?' 'Let the boy settle down first,' said his father, and he sat him on the bench behind the kitchen table. 'First have a drink and then we'll get you something to eat.' His family was obviously well provided with food, which his father obtained from the local farmers in exchange for carpentry work. Any initial uneasiness anyone may have felt about the family reunion soon faded, but his parents' inquisitive looks remained. But what could he tell them? He just didn't have the words to describe his experiences. They wouldn't understand what it was like out there, and he had no desire to bring the horror of the war into this world of tranquil naivety. A slight nod from his father gave him consent to continue when he started to tell some anecdotes about the daily routine of a soldier. Fascinated, his mother and sisters listened avidly as he described the war as if it was an adventure, exciting, tough and a bit dangerous, just like young men wished their lives to be.

Later, back in his own comfortable bed, the contradiction of lie and truth, of peace and war, wrestled within him. Uncertainty about his future strained at his nerves for hours, until he finally succumbed to a restless and all too short sleep. He woke up the next morning still exhausted, his head full of confused thoughts. He sought distraction by helping his father in the workshop, and finally found peace by concentrating on his familiar trade. His father didn't ask why he was silent, because he knew the inner tortures his son was going through. To him it was like yesterday as he remembered his own experience of returning home from the hell of front-line service for a few days a quarter of a century ago. He had gone to war rejoicing, but had come back subdued and wiser, brutally beaten by the merciless fist of reality. He could remember his feelings when confronted by the peace of home after experiencing the horror of war on the Italian front, his awareness of his family's ignorance of what he had gone through and his inability to find the words to tell them.

Father and son worked on silently in the workshop. Their movements were exact and in almost perfect harmony. There was an understanding between them that needed no words. They both knew about the experiences Sepp had left behind and his inability to confront the future. The inevitability of fate weighed heavily on everyone, but especially for a front-line soldier, whose life was reduced to the here and now, knowing that every mission could be his last. This knowledge determined the rhythm of his life.

The silence ended when his father looked into Sepp's eyes with a strange melancholy and said: 'Take care of yourself, boy, and come back healthy. You're needed here.'

The days passed and Sepp spent every one of them with his family. The village had become strange to him. His friends and schoolmates had all gone to the front, and many of them had fallen. Now everyone looked to the future with uncertainty and anxiety. The censored newspapers might untiringly express their belief in the Third Reich's ultimate victory, but meanwhile everybody could read between the lines. If they talked about 'elastic warfare on all fronts' it was clear to everyone that this meant 'withdrawal'. In the meantime the Western Allies had landed in France and opened a second front that called for so many forces that the army on the Eastern Front no longer received any reinforcements. Simultaneously, the Americans and British were increasing their pressure on the southern front in Italy while the Russians had commenced an offensive against Army Group Centre. With pressure on all fronts it was apparent that the Wehrmacht could not resist much longer. Complete, inescapable defeat was approaching. The attempt by some high-ranking Wehrmacht officers to kill Hitler and negotiate a separate peace failed, and Germany's fate was sealed.

Sepp's short leave came to an end. His father's features were set as if in stone as he shook his hand in farewell, but in a short embrace he felt him tremble with emotion. His mother and sisters cried their eyes out and were unable to find any words of encouragement. They were all in the hands of fate.

As Sepp's train rolled back towards the front line in Romania in the early days of August an inexplicable relief welled up inside him that he could go back to living and acting according to the archaic rules of war. While he was on leave Sepp had sensed unusual contradictions within him. The peace around him was not real. Life at home was characterized by uncertainty and fear of the unknown. At the front, by contrast, he knew what to do, knew his way around, and knew his soldier's trade. With this feeling came the certainty that he was ready to go on, all the way to the bitter end if necessary, with the troop of comrades that had become his home and family.

His return to Romania proceeded without incident, but he became aware that all the German soldiers he encountered on the way were anxious and restless. These were the dangerous early signs of demoralization. When he reached the last station Sepp and seven travelling companions were given a lift on an Opel Blitz that had been sent by his battalion to collect goods from the train. Sepp knew the driver, a lance corporal named Alois, who had served in GJR 144 for a long time. The closer they got to the front the stronger Sepp could feel the restlessness around him. Apart from wild latrine rumours he hadn't heard anything concrete, but Alois put him in the picture. 'Sepp, I tell you, there's something brewing. When I picked up the old man from the regiment I heard the officers talking about a message from the reconnaissance people. They think that a big offensive by Ivan is coming, and there's talk about our dear Romanian allies defecting, like the Hungarian secret service has reported. The shit has already started for Army Group Centre, and our Sixth Army is already in a real mess. They're about to be encircled. I tell you, something is going to happen in the next few days. They'll tear our arses up; there'll not be a dry eye in the place. Here, old boy, life is only bearable if you have some booze inside you.' With these words he got a bottle of fruit schnapps from under his seat. 'This is delicious stuff,' he said, clicking his tongue. 'I've stolen it from the regimental paymaster. That armchair farter got it in a parcel from his wife. Unfortunately it had a little "transport damage"! But he'll get over it – there were two bottles.' Sepp gladly took a mouthful and let the delicious, high-proof domestic fuel run down his throat with relish.

Their talk meandered for the rest of their ride, punctuated by occasional gulps from the bottle. Alois told Sepp that the past few weeks had been quiet and they'd enjoyed good summer weather. They were also getting on well with the neighbouring Romanian unit, and had received replacement personnel and supplies that brought Sepp's company nearly back to full fighting strength. When they finally reached II Battalion Alois asked Sepp if he wanted to visit the Romanians in the evening, since they had a good supply of booze from the local farmers. 'Sometimes there are even good-looking women. With a bit of talent, charm and a piece of bread you can fuck one of them.' 'First I've got to see how my people are,' said Sepp. 'I'll come over as soon as I can.' Then Sepp said goodbye and dutifully reported to battalion headquarters. He was welcomed by Captain Kloss with genuine pleasure. 'You've come back at just the right time. We can use every good man.' Then with a wink he added: 'Besides, you've probably become a good marksman by going on that gruelling course! There's a big push coming. Ivan will try to tear our arses up within the next few days.' That shrewd old devil Alois had been right, then, thought Sepp. 'Something's up with the Romanians as well,' Kloss continued. 'I think they're about to throw in the towel. The regimental staff officers have received a note from Foreign Armies East that according to Hungarian intelligence there's a Romanian opposition group emerging that wants to come to an arrangement with the Russians. High Command pays little attention to such intelligence, but personally I think there may be something to it. So do me a favour and keep away from the Romanians. There's something else.' He took a document and a brown paper bag from a pile of papers. 'Here's some more tinsel for your breast. Congratulations on being awarded your infantry assault badge.' He handed Sepp the certificate and medal, shook his hand and patted him on the back before turning back to his desk. 'Now, take a look round and we'll talk tomorrow.'

Sepp took his pack to the quarters of the runner he shared with and then went round the trenches looking for familiar faces. He hardly found any. Then a line from the song *Lilli Marlene* came to his mind: 'Tell me where the men are, over the trenches the wind blows.' The few remaining old hands seemed out of place among all the young newcomers, in whose juvenile faces Sepp believed he could see the shadow of death. He realized that after the next attack half of these new comrades would be missing too. When he met an old Landser it was less a case of joy at seeing each other again than a sense of relief and reassurance. They knew that they could rely on each other, which was a priceless feeling in battle. The newcomers, by contrast, had to provide proof of their reliability before they could be depended on.

At the end of his rounds Sepp visited the regimental Armourer. His first question was about the young marksman to whom he had passed his Russian rifle. 'That guy suffered a bad end,' the staff sergeant reported with a troubled expression. 'It's been quite peaceful here for the last few weeks, but there have been a few patrols around – you know, reconnaissance missions, taking prisoners for interrogation, sometimes a minor set-to just to keep the pressure on. The guy got too confident too soon. After a few days he went out alone, hunting and scouting. We don't know exactly what happened. Anyway, he went out in the evening and didn't come back. Four days later one of our patrols found his body, puffed up like a balloon by the heat. He must have fallen into the hands of a Russian patrol, and the stupid guy had obviously forgotten to get rid of his gun. You can imagine what Ivan does with a German marksman, especially one who has a captured Russian rifle and all those notches in the butt. They'd tortured him badly. He'd been beaten savagely and cut with knives. Finally they'd cut off his nuts and stuffed them into his mouth. But the worst thing was that they'd rammed his gun up his arse barrel first right up to the back sights. He must have died in agony. The comrades who found him in no-man's-land buried him there. When they got back they were all for setting out and taking revenge right then. Sepp, I tell you, this whole shit is getting too much for us. I don't want to think about what'll happen when Ivan gets into German territory. It's obvious that we've lost this war. All we can do is fight for survival now.' Putting his hand on Sepp's shoulder and looking into his eyes he added: 'But we'll do it like mountain riflemen should, to the very last cartridge and after that with our shovels and bare hands.'

Death was such a daily routine that Sepp was not too shaken by this episode, except by the brutal torture of the captured marksman. But it made him think. He swore never to cut notches into his rifle butt again and to do everything possible to conceal his identity as a marksman when there was any chance of being caught.

The pressure on the Carpathian front was increasing. The commanders of 3 Gebirgsjäger Division tried to secure their own sector as well as they could and integrated the neighbouring Romanian units into their defensive scheme. The Russian assault started a few days after Sepp's return and steadily increased in intensity. On 19 August 1944 the Russian artillery barrage became a wall of fire that was followed by a concerted attack. The Romanian units in the sector attacked were overrun without putting up any resistance and GJR 138 was encircled, though it managed to hold together. The division's few reserves were swiftly thrown in at some strategic risk, and after four days of violent fighting the encirclement around the 138th was broken and the front line was stabilized. Sepp's unit was barely involved in these battles except for skirmishes with Russian patrols.

Sepp was out and about almost every night reconnoitring ahead of the German lines, and he often observed small troops of the enemy disappearing amongst the positions held by neighbouring Romanian units. Strangely he never heard any sounds of fighting. His suspicions being aroused that a conspiracy was afoot, he reported his observations to Captain Kloss. 'Shit,' said Kloss, 'so there is something in the rumours. Sepp, now it starts. You'll see, the Romanians will stab us in the back.'

In wildly misjudged optimism, OKH denied that there was any danger of their Romanian allies defecting, despite the reports of commanders at the front. During the summer German suspicion of their allies had steadily increased as numerous small clues pointed to a change of heart amongst the Romanians. Commanders friendly to the Germans were replaced by others who did not like them, and the flow of Romanian intelligence to the Germans diminished and became contradictory. In addition the ordinary Romanian soldiers were burnt-out and tired of fighting even more than their German counterparts, because of their constant very heavy losses fighting on the Eastern Front with insufficient weapons. The approaching Russian attack on their home country was now anticipated with a sense of military impotence.

As the Russian offensive against Army Group Ukraine South commenced with the aim of encircling the Sixth Army, the two Romanian armies that should have defended their southern flank were beaten inside twenty-four hours and started a disordered retreat. Since the catastrophe of Stalingrad the Romanian government had been secretly negotiating with the Soviets for a separate armistice, though this had initially come to nothing because of the severe conditions set by the Russians. In June 1944 the various opposition factions within Romania were reconciled through the involvement of Romanian Communists and a plan was worked out for the overthrow of the Romanian fascist dictator Ion Antonescu and a break with Germany. Realistically assessing the hopelessness of the situation, King Michael of Romania agreed an armistice with the Allies and switched sides on 23 August. The same evening the Romanian Army received orders to cease hostilities against the Russians and to turn on the Germans. These orders were acted upon immediately. Contrary to the terms of the new Romanian-Russian pact the German ambassador and Wehrmacht supreme command in Romania were initially advised that the Germans troops would be given safe conduct out of the country with their weapons and equipment. Hitler, however, rejected any such arrangement and declared a state of war against Romania – another fatal mistake that further endangered Sixth Army's precarious position. Within hours, consequently, the Wehrmacht was involved in a war on two fronts that resulted in extraordinary losses in men and material that could not be replaced, and utter disruption of their front. By 30 August Army Group Ukraine South had been almost destroyed. Supreme Headquarters in Berlin could follow events by simply moving and removing flags on a map, but the Landsers had to face the music of the Führer's heroic decisions on the ground.

For the riflemen of 3 GD the fighting situation was complicated. Not only had they two enemies now, but the Romanian people themselves divided into those who supported their government's new alliance with the Russians – the future partisans against the Wehrmacht – and those soldiers and civilians who remained loyal to the Nazi cause and tagged along behind the Germans. This confusion was to lead to a multitude of unfortunate and tragic incidents.

23 August itself was a bright summer's day and there was no real fighting going on in GJR 144's sector. Even so, the Germans' nerves were on edge because of the depressing situation. At midday Sepp met Alois the driver again, who was serving as a regimental runner. 'What's up, poacher?' said Alois. 'Want a drink tonight? Our Romanians have received some new stuff and invited us over. Don't be shy – come along.' Sepp was curious, and a swig was not to be sneezed at, so he agreed. Alois described the place and the way to the Romanian unit and said goodbye through his cab window: 'See you tonight at about eight, so don't let 'em shoot you until then.'

It was almost 21:00 on this fateful day when Sepp strolled through the forest towards their meeting place with his gun over his shoulder. Although the fighting line was about 2km away he was constantly attentive to his surroundings, which had often saved his life. Thus it was that he became aware of a strange background noise shortly before he reached the Romanian positions, which lay beyond the next curve along the track. An incomprehensible and excited babble of voices broke the tranquillity of the evening air. Instantly alert, Sepp left the track and disappeared into the undergrowth, doubling back to a little rise from where he hoped to see the Romanian positions. His senses taut, he crept like a cat in the direction of the noises and carefully pushed his way through the thick bushes to the top of the rise. From here he had a view across a valley as wide as a football field in which the Romanian troops were encamped. About a hundred metres away, at a junction of the forest track he had just left, Sepp saw Alois and four other Landsers through his binoculars, surrounded by Romanians and two Russians. The Landsers were tied up and about to be interrogated. The Russians were talking to the Romanians, whereupon one of these asked the prisoners some questions. The answers did not seem to satisfy their captors, because one of the Russians pushed the Romanian aside and started to beat the riflemen with a stick. In the meantime there was a larger group of Romanians looking on, and Sepp could tell by their behaviour that they were unhappy about what the Russian was doing. Then an officer appeared and reprimanded the onlookers to no effect before finally pulling out his pistol, whereupon the Romanians shuffled back to their positions lashed by the tongues of their NCOs. Then the officer talked with the interrogation group and they moved off, apparently to continue their questioning in less exposed surroundings.

At the bottom of the slope, right below Sepp's position, there was a latrine. The interrogators and their prisoners went round behind the back wall so that they could no longer be seen from the camp, and this allowed Sepp an even clearer view of them. The distance was about 80m. Besides the five captives there were now two Russians and three Romanians. One Romanian was interpreting; the other two were there as guards. Once again the Russians started to hit the riflemen. Amidst the noise of this beating odd words and phrases reached Sepp's ears, like 'dirty pig' and 'traitor', and he recognised Alois's voice. Now the Russians began to concentrate their attention on Alois. They beat him harder with their sticks, and then one Russian and one Romanian started to punch him in the face and stomach, so that he fell to the ground doubled up with pain. Then they loosened his bonds and dragged him to the latrine wall, where they pressed his right hand against a beam and the leading Russian took out his pistol and used it against Alois's fingers like a hammer. Alois screamed in a mixture of rage and pain as his fingertips were beaten one by one to a bloody mush. Sepp was almost overwhelmed by fury and a wild urge to take action. But experience had taught him to control such impulses and to wait for the right moment. A hasty reaction might endanger both his own safety and the lives of his comrades, since there was still a chance that the prisoners might just be marched off into captivity when this was all over. So Sepp calmed himself and continued to watch, though all the time thinking feverishly about how and when he might be able to help his comrades. There was no point in running back to the German positions to form a patrol and take on the entire Romanian detachment – firstly because it was improbable that they would recover the prisoners alive, secondly because it would cost even more German lives, and thirdly because the defection of the entire Romanian armed forces was expected imminently. So it seemed to Sepp that there was only one solution: it was up to him.

In order to suppress his screams, Alois was gagged. His torturers had clearly believed that seeing his suffering would encourage the other prisoners to provide them with the information they wanted, but questioning them did not bring the results they hoped for, even when the fingertips of Alois's left hand were smashed too. Moaning, he rolled through the dust while his companions were beaten and questioned in turn. Sepp had meanwhile prepared a rest for his carbine and got into firing position. He was ready to shoot, but he still hoped that the Russians would give up torturing their victims and lead them off into captivity. A misguided hope, as it turned out. With sudden amazement he noticed the Russian with the pistol suddenly tear open Alois's jacket and trousers so that his stomach shone pale and white in the gathering gloom. Suddenly the Russian pulled a knife from his jacket, opened the blade and waved it threateningly in the faces of the other four Landsers as they knelt on the ground. He screamed at them, and the interpreting Romanian gesticulated wildly and spoke rapidly before finally shrugging his shoulders in resignation. With that the Russian turned back to Alois and with a sudden movement cut open his abdominal wall below the navel, thrust his hand into the wound and pulled out about a metre of his intestines. Alois's moan of agony was clearly audible despite his gag.

Sepp was used to seeing horrrible things in this war, but this utterly sickened him. His heart beat so furiously he thought it would burst and helpless rage overwhelmed him. The moment to act had come. The Russian's brutality had even shocked the Romanian interpreter, who suddenly got his own pistol out and relieved Alois's suffering by two rapid shots to the head. The situation suddenly escálated. Both Russians now had their guns out, and they and the Romanians were threatening and screaming at each other. The Russian torturer waved his pistol at the interpreter and then suddenly turned towards the kneeling prisoners and fired into the first one's face. A spray of blood and tissue exploded from the back of the Landser's head. For seconds he knelt there like a statue, then he tipped over sideways onto the legs of his comrades.

Sepp had regained his composure in the meantime. Rage had given way to his hunter's instincts. He already had the Russian in his reticle. A short breath, concentration, and then his finger took the pressure point and squeezed. The shot hit the torturer's breast like an iron fist and threw him backwards. Sepp was ready again even as his first victim hit the ground, and the second Russian fell victim to his next bullet. The Romanian interpreter realized what was happening instantly and leapt over the latrine wall in a single bound: there was a splash of shit as he landed in the well-filled hole. The two remaining Romanians fired wildly into the forest without their bullets coming anywhere near Sepp, whose third shot threw one of them against the wall. In the meantime the whole Romanian camp was abuzz with excitement. Smeared with shit from head to foot the interpreter ran out of the latrine. The first machine guns were firing into the forest now, their hail of bullets coming dangerously close to Sepp. He could not help the surviving riflemen. He had to escape as quickly as he could in order to warn his comrades. Like a ghost he disappeared inside the forest.

When he reached the Gebirgsjäger positions there was already hectic activity. He went immediately to Captain Kloss and reported what he had seen in short sentences. Although he left out the details Kloss could imagine what had happened. 'Damn,' he hissed, and he set about trying to get into radio contact with regimental headquarters and the neighbouring units. It turned out that the Romanians had already attacked in some places and had captured two of the battalion's detachments. Sepp's report merely provided the final proof that the Romanians were now their enemies.

Regimental headquarters was unable to offer any recommendations and could do no more than seek guidance from divisional headquarters. Next Kloss contacted III Battalion of Gebirgs Artillerie Regiment 112, but immediately after that the radio network was sabotaged. Then each unit was on its own, as had so often been the case during the past few months. But Kloss's battalion was lucky things did not turn out worse. They reacted immediately because they were warned sufficiently early, and every company was put on the alert to defend itself against Romanian encroachments.

But many others units suffered badly. The Romanians approached the generally unsuspecting Germans with what appeared to be friendly intentions and then struck murderously. Romanian combat groups coalesced that were similar to partisan groups, led by infiltrated Russian agents. Acting with extreme harshness and brutality, these spread panic among the German units, who were unable to tell friend from foe. While other units had to take bitter losses, the riflemen of II/GJR 144 defended themselves with grim determination. When groups of Romanians approached their positions with the usual familiarity but their weapons handy, the forewarned riflemen fired at their first suspicious movement, though such situations became a whole lot trickier when they took place at night. Fortunately the Romanians had no heavy weapons and the superior firepower of the riflemen gave them the edge when it came to firefights. So it was that GJR 144 became 3 GD's centre of resistance and the rallying point for its tactical and strategic reorganization. Survivors of the division's other shattered elements fought their way to the 144th and provided the necessary reinforcements to mount counterstrikes to rescue other surrounded units. By the next morning assault groups had already been put together and were advancing against the Romanians. Filled with rage and indignation at their betrayal and seeking revenge for the Romanians' violence towards their former allies, the riflemen stormed into them like berserkers. The German counterattacks were savage and took no prisoners, since the necessary logistical support had been destroyed. Sepp served as an ordinary rifleman during this confused fighting, since his marksman's rifle would just have got in the way. Instead he fought with a self-loading rifle Model 43 that he'd obtained on his return from leave, though he'd had to watch it like a hawk to make sure no one pilfered it. At distances up to about a hundred metres and loaded with explosive bullets, this had considerable striking power.

Within a few days the division had managed to drive the Romanians from its sector and to stabilize its positions. But it was quite alone. During the same period Sixth Army was almost completely destroyed. At the same time the Russians stormed Bucharest and the southern oil fields of Ploesti. This left 3 GD's positions projecting into the Russian front like a thorn. Consequently the Russians attacked them next following their success against Sixth

Army in the north. On 27 August the intensity of the Soviet attacks increased beyond their usual skirmishes and became a major offensive against all the Carpathian passes that the division held.

II Battalion had a special importance in these battles, because it was utilized as a sort of fire brigade, being thrown in wherever the need was greatest. Its riflemen were able to repel the enemy again and again, because they were fighting over terrain they had come to know well and, being in their element as trained mountain troops, they enjoyed a clear tactical advantage over the Russians. Yet though they fought with all their might the vortex of events around them was spinning faster and faster and gradually it sucked them in. The regimental histories might have unemotionally and rationally recorded these battles in tones of bombastic optimism – General Klatt, for instance, wrote: 'In the virgin Carpathians the riflemen felt strong and free, in harmony with the mountains. If the time really had come for all Hell to break loose, then why should fate not dictate that they die right there?' – but reality was more unpleasant. The Gebirgstruppen didn't die in a painted sunset, to the sound of music in the spicy mountain air, and by a clean shot through the heart and a sudden death. No, death was always dirty, stinking, and tore bodies to twitching, blood-spattered shreds of flesh. Every day could be a soldier's last and the fear of death, mutilation and the uncertainty of Russian imprisonment consumed everyone. But they either learned to live with the insanity, or they were dead within a few days. And despite everything they continued to hope.

The Eastern Front was by now devouring up to forty Landsers a day – a casualty rate that Germany could no longer sustain. The army's logistics had already failed as early as the winter of 1941–42, and by the autumn of 1944 were no more than makeshift. Again and again the riflemen had to give up captured territory simply because their supplies failed. Even their medical supplies were increasingly interrupted by the constant fluctuations of the front line, and organized evacuation of the wounded was often impossible. A serious wound at the front was virtually a death sentence.

Chapter 13

Another anonymous statistic

Many of 3 GD's units were encircled by the Romanians and Russians in the closing days of August but fought grimly on. The 144th did what it could to assist these pockets of resistance, mounting courageous attacks that often broke through and enabled their trapped comrades to escape. Sepp accompanied a patrol sent out to relieve a small detachment that had been defending a pass against the Russians for three days and had been cut off from retreat by Romanian troops. The Romanians consisted of ten men with sub-machine guns and carbines. Though numerically inferior to the defenders they could prevent their escape because of their superb field of fire and cleverly chosen positions. The Romanians themselves clearly felt safe and did not expect to be attacked. Luckily the advance of the German patrol was concealed by thick undergrowth and went unseen by the Romanians, whose whereabouts were unknown to them. When Sepp and the patrol sergeant finally spotted them through their binoculars it was with some relief that they realized their arrival had not been detected. This provided them with the decisive element of surprise. Throwing grenades and following them with volleys of machine-pistol fire and well-aimed carbine shots, the Romanians were annihilated within seconds. There was no escape. But this success didn't solve the problem yet, for an open field still lay between themselves and the cut-off detachment, which was clearly visible to the Russians and within easy reach of their weapons.

Alerted by the sound of gunfire to their rear, the seven remaining defenders now realized that unlooked for help was close at hand. Through his binoculars Sepp saw them talking and gesticulating to each other. But how could they reach them? Then, while defenders and relief force alike considered their options, there suddenly came the whooshing sounds of Russian heavy mortars which shattered the silence. The Soviets had finally brought up heavy weapons to clear the pass. The patrol members threw themselves flat and hugged the ground, but the salvo was aimed at the defensive positions rather than them. With dull thuds the exploding shells burst across the ground, the wall of fire rolling steadily towards the German positions. In his binoculars Sepp saw the defenders' faces distorted by panic. The patrol that had hoped to relieve them was unable to do anything. The defenders now had no more than the slimmest of chances to escape certain death by flight across the open ground to their rear. The patrol could only look on helplessly. Shortly before the first mortar shells hit their positions the seven men jumped up and sprinted across the field – to be knocked down by well-aimed gunshots in their backs one after another. Instead of zigzagging they had tried to reach the forest in a straight line. Sepp immediately recognized the signature of a Russian marksman equipped with a Tokarev 40 self-loading gun. He had seen these weapons and had even tried out a captured example. It wasn't as precise as a repeater like the German Model 43, but it was reliable and improved an experienced marksman's rate of fire considerably. Sepp had learned from his battalion Armourer that there was a marksman's version of this weapon with a telescopic sight similar to the one on his original Russian rifle.

The next salvo of mortar fire ploughed up the German positions and tore the fallen riflemen apart, burying most of them beneath a shower of stones and soil. Then there was a sudden silence, broken by the screams of the few injured men still alive. Two members of the patrol volunteered to make a rescue attempt, and carefully using what little cover there was they worked their way forward to their comrades. When they reached the first of them, one of the rescuers raised himself a little higher than was wise and was immediately hit in the breast by a bullet. Through his glasses Sepp saw a fountain of blood spray from him for several seconds. Obviously the Russian sniper's explosive bullet had destroyed an artery near to the heart. The rifleman's body trembled and twitched in his death throes. Sepp desperately scanned the Russian positions, but they remained hidden and unreachable by the riflemen's weapons. The presence of the Russian marksman meant that another attempt to rescue their comrades was hopeless. Only by luck was the second rifleman able to get back unhurt. Meanwhile the screams and moans of the injured faded away as death released them, except for one, who from the

Landsers' experience they knew had been hit in a kidney. His agonized screaming was only interrupted by short periods when he slipped into unconsciousness. But he clung desperately to life and the hope of rescue. Yet no matter how the patrol looked at the situation, there was no way to rescue him without risking more lives. Now the screams broke off and they heard the wounded man call feebly for help. The men saw him raise one hand, seeking help. Seconds later the hand was torn off by a shot from the Russian marksman's rifle. Bloodily shredded like a broken branch, the stump continued to wave in the air. The Russian sniper obviously wanted to teach the Landsers a lesson in horror.

Again the screams began. The sergeant waved Sepp over to him, put his hand on his shoulder and looked at him gravely. 'I can't force you, I can only beg you, and I know that what I ask is a very hard thing, but I beg you – release our comrade with a decent shot. You're the only one who can do it at that distance.'

This was a situation Sepp had always dreaded would come. He had often seen the Russians shoot their wounded comrades in no-man's-land. But on the German side such behaviour was unusual, because such systematic killing would have seriously demoralized their men. It was an unwritten rule in the Wehrmacht to always rescue injured men if possible. The only exception was mercy killing carried out at the request of wounded men in hopeless situations. Sepp had shuddered when he'd seen this done during the past few months, when terribly wounded soldiers who couldn't be moved begged comrades to kill them to spare them any further suffering. It was expected that men left behind would be tortured and killed by the Soviets, since it wasn't feasible for enemy assault troops to give them any help.

Sepp was still hesitating, but the others urged him to do what the sergeant asked. 'Come on, man, do something. You can't leave him like that. Shit, release the poor devil.' Unwillingly, beset by his scruples, Sepp rested his carbine on a rolled tent square. The distance was about 80m, but the wounded man's head was hidden in the grass and his body was partly concealed by a fold in the ground and several large stones. Sepp tried to aim carefully, but he was trembling at the thought of what he was about to do, and a choke of emotion welled up inside him.

Suddenly he became aware of the monstrousness, the absurdness, of war, and the constant pointless killing. Fighting had now become an end in itself. But now that the anonymity of his target could not salve his conscience, he had real scruples for the first time about what he did. He felt a wave of compassion course through him and sought for answers that didn't exist. He had allowed the momentum of war to subdue his morality beneath its yoke. Like many others he had resigned himself to his duty as a sniper because of honest patriotism, and with that duty he had accepted his fate, mortgaging his future peace of mind by accepting indelible responsibility for his selfless duty.

It took mere seconds for these wildly circling thoughts to race through his mind, but it seemed like an eternity to him. Then he arrived at the only possible decision – to bring a swift end to his comrade's suffering. Sepp forced himself to be calm, loaded a B-cartridge, took aim at the twitching head, and waited for a chance to shoot. Suddenly the wounded man's body stiffened and his scream became hoarse. His head was still. Sepp's sight settled on the ear of the dying man and with a slight tremble of his finger Sepp pulled the trigger. Their comrade's head burst in a bloody fountain and a paralyzing silence descended.

The Russians went quiet. Obviously they hadn't expected such a course of action and had decided it was safer to stay where they were. The riflemen took advantage of this breathing space to slip away undisturbed. No one said anything and nobody looked at each other. Silent and subdued the Landsers crept away, each of them relieved that it was not he who had had to do it. It was the marksman who'd done what was necessary and now paid the price of inner conflict and isolation. Over the next few days they continued to search for pockets of resistance in need of rescue, but their failure in the pass, minor episode of war though it was, would haunt Sepp in a strange way for the rest of his days.

Soon after their return he was ordered to accompany another patrol seeking a cut-off detachment. By now the course of the front line had become quite confused, and they had to cross a minefield on the way. The previous day a group of pioneers had cleared a narrow path through the mines and marked it with small sticks. Despite this they felt uneasy and crept along almost on tiptoe and with their breath held.

About ninety minutes later they had crossed the minefield and had carefully worked their way through a stretch of undergrowth. The old hands among them had developed a feel for the ground and for danger, so the patrol's advance guard was already on the alert when it encountered another unexpected minefield, this time fitted with tripwires. These always indicated there was a Russian position nearby. Carefully using every bit of cover available they tried to go around the minefield, but this proved more problematic and time-consuming than they had anticipated. In the meantime dusk had come down and they were obliged to withdraw, since moving about in a minefield in the dark was extremely dangerous. But before they did, the patrol leader wanted to take a look from a nearby hilltop and he waved Sepp over to join him. From here they had a clear view of the well-built Russian positions. While they observed these through their binoculars Sepp noticed a movement in the bushes about 20m away and saw a pale-coloured patch in the gloom. Looking closer he saw that it was a squatting Russian with his pants down, relieving himself. 'Sepp, do you see that, too?' whispered the sergeant. 'There's an Ivan over there squatting and shitting. If you can hit him the others will get a proper fright. They think we're in a totally different area. I'll get back to the others. Put off your shot for as long as possible, and then follow me.' His comrade disappeared and Sepp took the Russian into his crosshairs. 'Let him lay down the muck, then he's due,' Sepp thought. Suddenly a cynical comic rhyme came into his head: 'The lightning shall hit while you shit.' The wit of war.

The distance was about 150m. To be sure of hitting his enemy in the breast he aimed at his throat. Then he breathed deeply, concentrated, and fired. At the very same moment the Russian got up, so the projectile hit his lower abdomen, sliced through his intestines and left his body via a big hole in his back. He cried like an animal in utter panic. Startled by the shot, his comrades emerged from their dugout and returned a wild, unaimed fire. Sepp crawled away backwards and hurried after his comrades.

At the crack of dawn the next day they were on their way again to look for their missing comrades. But now they had another order too. If possible they should capture a Russian and bring him back for interrogation. Using paths they knew well they crept towards the enemy. The Russians in turn seemed to have decided to get a better idea of their enemy's positions, but they set out later than the riflemen and the two patrols encountered one another just ahead of the Soviet lines. Since the Landsers were moving more carefully they spotted the Russians first, so they had the advantage of surprise on their side. In addition they were equipped with another new gun that had only become available in small numbers over the past few weeks. This was the Sturmgewehr 44, which was a cross between a machine-pistol and a carbine, with a lever which switched it from semi-automatic to fully automatic mode. It fired a special shortened carbine cartridge called Pistolenpatrone 43, the magazine holding thirty rounds. This ammunition had sufficient power to travel up to 300m. The Sturmgewehr was also more comfortable to fire than a 98k carbine, because the cartridge was weaker and part of its recoil energy was used in the automatic reload process, whereas the powerful recoil of the 98k led to painful bruises in the shoulder after forty or fifty shots even amongst men used to using it. This was one reason why few hits were scored with the 98k in battle, because soldiers were more concerned with avoiding the recoil than in firing well-aimed shots.

In the ensuing short and violent fight with the Russian patrol the Sturmgewehrs proved their worth. Within a few minutes all their enemies were dead or seriously wounded without any loss on their own side. They had been so thorough, in fact, that there were no survivors fit enough to be taken back for questioning. The riflemen had no qualms about dealing with the wounded Russians. A hard-boiled Landser insensitive about such things shot the few Russians still alive with his pistol while the rest of the patrol searched the dead for usable information in the form of paybooks, passes and identification cards bearing tactical insignia. But the Russians interrupted proceedings with heavy mortar fire from their nearby positions, without any consideration for their comrades, and the riflemen had to depart as quickly as possible. They dashed along the edge of the minefield they had discovered the previous day and into a bushy area, from which, after going a few hundred metres, they suddenly saw the position occupied by the comrades they had been looking for. But they saw immediately that they were all dead. After having fired their last rounds they had obviously been killed in hand-to-hand combat. They scanned the position from a group of bushes, fuller and closer examination not being possible because there was so little cover between them and the Russian lines. In addition they could hear noises nearby, and had to assume that the enemy was somewhere in the immediate vicinity.

While Sepp observed the area through his binoculars something caught his eye. There it was. A brand new Gebirgsjäger cap, its tin edelweiss badge shining in the sun. He glanced up at the tattered peak of his own totally worn-out cap and immediately decided to retrieve the other one as a replacement. He crept carefully towards the object of his desire. There were just a few metres to go when he suddenly saw the body of the comrade to whom the cap had belonged. His blank eyes were staring at the sky, and his chest was torn apart by so many splinters that bits of rib were poking out. Hundreds of flies were swarming around the corpse. The chain of his identity disc had slipped up around his ears and the discs lay beside his head. When Sepp reached him he put his own cap over the dead man's face and put on the new one. He was pleased to find that it fitted perfectly. At that moment he heard a vehicle approaching and realized it was high time to leave. The thought of taking the dead man's ID tags didn't come to him until it was too late. By the time he thought of it he was in the bushes and the Russian vehicle was too close, so he couldn't go back. And with that the dead soldier became just another anonymous statistic in the list of men missing in action. It would have taken only a moment to grab the tags so that the man's relatives could have known his fate. But all Sepp had thought about was the new cap. This unintentional act of selfishness haunted him for the rest of his life.

As the whole of Romania became caught up in the bitter fighting only the resolutely defended positions of 3 GD stood in the way of the mighty Red Army. Despite its inferiority in men and material the division held on for as long as possible so that the German front line could be restabilized, but the Soviets were eventually able to push their way through by sheer weight of numbers. The Germans therefore resorted to ambush tactics as the Russians tried to advance through the narrow mountain passes. The conditions were ideal for marksmen, who were able to prepare well-camouflaged positions overlooking the enemy's known route of advance and to fire at him at pre-determined ranges. Even with inferior forces the German defence was consequently successful, because the enemy could not deploy to make best use of his numerical superiority within the confines of the narrow valleys, but instead had to fight his way through metre by metre and suffered heavy losses accordingly. Sepp scored up to twenty hits a day in these battles, although few of them found their way into his official total.

It was in early September that Kloss showed Sepp a circular from OKH concerning Wehrmacht and Waffen-SS marksmen. By order of the Führer a special Marksman's Badge had been introduced in three grades. The first grade was awarded for twenty confirmed kills, the second, with a silver cord, for forty kills, and the third, with a gold cord, for sixty kills. The new embroidered oval badge should be worn on the right forearm of the uniform jacket above any other badges. But obviously, no sane marksman would ever wear such a badge in battle. The meaning of the badge would soon have become known to the enemy, so that wearing one would have been tantamount to suicide.

As before, kills in straightforward fighting did not count towards these badges, and Heinrich Himmler decreed that all kills scored up to that time had to be erased from the record as a gift to the Führer. Counting had to start again from scratch. However, as a reward for their good work the marksmen were each to receive an Iron Cross Second Class, or First Class if they already possessed a second class cross. Sepp received his own Iron Cross Second Class a few days later.

In reality this official recognition of marksmen, who had been reviled up till then, resulted from the steadily diminishing output of the German armaments industry, and was clearly intended to encourage the stalwart resistance of such lone warriors. Armed with no more than a rifle, and with no regard for their personal safety, it was hoped that such men might be able to compensate for the army's ever-increasing lack of weapons and equipment.

At the same time as the Soviets maintained their pressure on the virtually impregnable positions of the riflemen, they managed to break through into Hungary in another sector. As a result encirclement once again threatened 3 Gebirgsjäger Division, and it was left with no choice but to abandon its positions and withdraw to the River Maros, 200km away. The riflemen pulled back as quickly as they could, marching by night and fighting holding actions against their Russian pursuers by day. While the battalion marched, Kloss hurried ahead to plan out their positions for the next day. Sepp had to accompany him, because Kloss regarded him as an experienced and tough soldier on whom he could depend. He was something like a bodyguard for Kloss.

As a regular officer Kloss had been taught to ride during his training, so in order to travel cross-country without giving himself away by the noise of an engine he took to riding a horse during his daily explorations. Sepp therefore had to be mounted too, and rode one of the tough Panje steppe horses that had formed the backbone of the Wehrmacht's logistical effort on the Eastern Front since 1943. Unlike his commander, however, Sepp had no experience of riding beyond owning a rocking horse as a child. So when he swung himself up on the unsaddled horse for the first time it was with very mixed emotions. He sprawled across its back like an ape, pressing his legs together as tightly as he could to hold himself in place. Despite that, however, he bounced about like a rubber ball as the horse moved, and he saw a glint of malicious humour in Kloss's eyes as he waited for him to fall off. But Sepp was determined not to show himself up and he bravely clung on for the entire ride, which lasted about an hour. After exploring the new positions he begged that he might take the job of rearguard, because there was no way he could have made it back on the horse – the rough cloth of his uniform had rubbed his crotch raw on the ride out. When the rest of the unit eventually came up he immediately visited the battalion doctor and asked for his discreet help in a delicate matter. The doctor gave him a tin of Penaten cream to ease his immediate discomfort, but under no circumstances could he get back on a horse for the next few days. Grinning widely Kloss simulated sympathy and switched to a BMW bike and sidecar for his scouting missions. Kloss occupied the sidecar while Sepp sat in the pillion seat behind the rider. He left his gun behind because his back had been badly bruised by the carbine repeatedly hitting him as he bounced about on the horse. In its place he carried an MP40.

Rattling along the road they met an infantry combat group that was also withdrawing and was accompanied by two assault guns that were still fit to fight. Talking to the officers, Kloss learned that a patrol had seen a Russian tank somewhere along this road, so a high degree of caution was called for. A few minutes later they rode on, and just as they passed the foremost assault gun it suddenly stopped and fired. The motorcycle was hardly 2m from the muzzle at the time, and Sepp felt as if a bomb had exploded in his head. Blinded by the muzzle flash, he was thrown from the saddle and into the bushes at the side of the road and was briefly knocked out. When he came to several seconds later he was lying in the grass with every bone in his body aching, his head ringing and his ears whistling. Directly in front of him the motorcycle rider was rolling around likewise concussed, while Kloss sat alone in the sidecar gawking at them. They were all too shell-shocked to move as a short fight with the Russian vanguard unfolded around them. The enemy soon pulled back and the riflemen received help a few minutes later. But it took them more than half an hour to recover sufficiently to continue on their way, and it took days for the whistling in Sepp's ears to stop.

It was not this episode that forced him back onto a horse, but the general circumstances that now prevailed at the front. By 1944 the German army was dependent on hundreds of thousands of horses to maintain its ailing logistics and guarantee it any form of mobility. Lack of petrol, huge losses, and insufficient standardization of parts had resulted in the number of serviceable vehicles declining dramatically. Infantry units in particular were often without any motor vehicles at all. Thus it was that the hard-working and genial Panje horses became so essential to the German army's logistical survival.

So making a virtue of necessity, Sepp sought instruction from a comrade who had been a farmer and knew about horses, and after about a week of practice he was able to ride sufficiently well that he got through the remainder of his cavalry excursions without further mishap.

Soon afterwards a supply lorry reached them with a few replacements and some much-needed ammunition. Sepp received a message from the battalion weapons and equipment sergeant saying that he had exciting news and that Sepp should come and see him. When he got there he saw before him ten brand new Model 43 self-loading rifles and three small green-painted boxes containing 4x Model ZF 41 sights. The sergeant had received written orders from the battalion Armourer to fit the sights to the three most accurate of the new weapons and mark each mounting with its rifle's serial number. Knowing that Sepp had handled such weapons and sights on his marksman's course, he told him that he needed his help to check the rifles and pick out the best three. Finding the best three didn't take long, but when Sepp was offered one of them he declined, because the ZF 41 sight was inferior to the one on his K98k, whether it be in brightness, optical clarity, or range of vision. But he nevertheless asked the sergeant to hold back one of the guns for him, since he recognized its tactical advantages in certain fighting situations. A couple of proven sharpshooters received the other two weapons. But marking the mountings with the rifles' serial numbers proved to be quite difficult, the special steel from which they were manufactured being so hard that the numbers they stamped on were barely legible.

After a hard night march the riflemen picked out their new positions in the early morning light and dug themselves in. The Russians were hard on their heels and they were expecting the first patrols at any moment. Sepp accompanied Captain Kloss on a last informal inspection of the defences. Suddenly a single shot whizzed through the morning silence and hit a machine-gun position about 5m ahead of them. Ducking down, they sprinted to the trench, where a rifleman sat holding his cap in his hand, its edelweiss badge ripped off. Sepp recognized the signs instantly: a Russian marksman. The Landser, having been at the front for only a few days, saw his commander and wanted to report where the shot had come from. Before Sepp could stop him he had risen again to point over the edge of the trench, but the first word was not out of his mouth before Sepp had leapt at him and thrown him to the ground. At the very same moment the Russian fired again, and his shot glanced across the top of the falling rifleman's head. Blood sprayed everywhere as the bullet tore a piece of bone from the left side of his skull. Despite the severity of his wound the Landser did not lose consciousness. Sepp and the second machine gunner took the field-dressing from his pocket and bandaged him. Then Kloss took him back to the battalion aid station. All the while he stuttered: 'What's happened? Who hit me? Am I hurt?' Then he suddenly looked at Kloss wide-eyed and asked: 'Dad, will you take me home now? Mum will be waiting for us!' It sent a shiver down Kloss's spine, but he answered: 'Stay calm, lad. You just fell down. We'll go home now and everything will be fine.'

Sepp stayed in the machine-gun position. Word that there was a Russian sniper somewhere spread like wildfire through the riflemen's lines, and they became alarmed. They looked to Sepp to solve the problem for them. Marksmen were repeatedly put under this sort of pressure. The officers in particular always expected them to fearlessly and successfully execute every task with which they were presented, regardless of feasibility. If the marksman succeeded, he'd just done his job. But if he failed, he was often reviled for cowardice or incompetence. Yet he could not perform miracles every time, especially when fighting against enemy marksmen. Though Sepp had sometimes sensed such unpleasant pressure, he was lucky enough to have unusually sensible superiors.

Whenever possible he constructed himself a well-camouflaged

observation post each time the unit moved to new positions, and he moved to the one he'd prepared here as soon as a replacement machine gunner arrived to relieve him. From there he hoped to trace the Soviet. But his opponent was a cunning devil, because suddenly he had just vanished. The day passed in strained watchfulness but nothing more happened, and in the evening the riflemen once again abandoned their positions just as the first Russian machine guns started barking across no-man's-land.

A few days later they came to the wooded valley of the River Maros. Kloss's daily reconnaissance of their next defensive position was over and Sepp was trotting along surrounded by his comrades. All of them were chronically overtired and they were walking as if they were in a trance. Only the guard detachments remained alert. A vanguard of five men was marching about 50m ahead of them. Suddenly a dull explosion roused the riflemen from their exhaustion. Everybody was immediately awake, and they all leapt for cover. Jumping into a ditch Sepp saw one of his comrades being thrown down by the explosion and hit by a second detonation as he struck the ground. Sepp realized instantly that this was no ambush: the rifleman had stepped on a mine. His warning spread rapidly among the survivors, and everybody began to edge their way forward as carefully as possible. Since Sepp was at the front he worked his way over to the wounded man with a medical orderly. In the gleam of his flashlight the dying man's face shone white as chalk. No sound came from his lips, and his eyes were already staring unfocussed at the threshold of eternity. The first mine had torn off his lower left leg, and when he had hit the ground his backside had detonated the second mine, which had blown apart his behind and his thighs. The bloody tissue was trembling like jelly. Small fountains of blood throbbed from his ruptured arteries. Splintered bones poked out from the deadly wounds. Even as they reached him, the mortally injured rifleman sighed, gave a last convulsive shudder, and died.

In this war there was no time for ritual any more. The dead soldier was just a corpse, and they left him where he fell. The medical orderly just took his identity disc. The rest of the troop had meanwhile formed a single file behind two men on all fours who carefully searched the ground ahead for further mines. It later transpired that they had walked into a minefield laid by withdrawing Hungarian troops to cover their own retreat. It took the riflemen more than five hours to cover a few hundred metres, with everybody trying to follow in exactly the same footsteps as the man in front, but they got through without any further losses. Fortunately such encounters with mines were rather rare. Since the Germans were constantly retreating it was primarily they who laid minefields, in order to delay the pursuing Russians, while the swiftly advancing Soviets rarely felt the need to safeguard their own positions in this way.

This incident reawakened the riflemen from their apathy, and thereafter they kept their eyes peeled for evidence of mines. When they reached their new positions they saw that one bushy section was strewn with suspicious little mounds that indicated something being buried. They knew that an Hungarian regiment had been stationed in this area, so they assumed the worst and taped the area off as a warning to the rest of the battalion that was following behind them. Since the area could not be left out of the defensive scheme, it was decided to partially clear it, and under the guidance of pioneers teams were formed to remove the mines. They crept in on all fours and began to prod the suspicious mounds with their fingers and the tips of their bayonets. Suddenly several riflemen let out howls of disgust. The mines turned out to be piles of shit. They were in a latrine, not a minefield!

The division had hardly reached its new front line positions around Deda in Hungary when the enemy attacked in strength, maintaining a concerted offensive against the riflemen's positions from 24 September until 8 October. These hard-fought battles resulted in many losses, but the Gebirgsjäger managed to break the attack and maintain their positions. However, the Soviets succeeded in breaking through south of 3 GD, and with the integrity of the front line again compromised the division had to abandon the positions it had sacrificed so many lives to defend. It fell back to a new defensive line along the River Theiss.

The situation was complicated by the fact that Hungary was no longer a reliable ally. Its political factions had polarized and parts of its army had defected to the Russians, though other units remained unconditionally loyal to the Germans. Further decisive weakening of the German front was inevitable under these circumstances. It was now that Sepp and his comrades began to see columns of civilian refugees fleeing alongside the withdrawing Wehrmacht units, not just people of German origin but also many Hungarians opposed to

Communism. With that the war became even more stressful, because these civilians often got caught up in the fighting and the Landsers were unable to help them, and had to watch them suffer and die too. With that every soldier ceased to see any sense of duty in what he did. The fighting had been reduced to a mere struggle for survival.

On the huge Hungarian plains known as the Pussta, the numerically superior Russian armoured units developed their offensive. In order to maintain contact with the main body of the retreating German army, Combat Group Wöhler, to which 3 Gebirgsjäger Division belonged, had to drive a path through the Russians to the town of Nyiregyhaza. Bitter battles developed, into which the columns of refugees were drawn without mercy. Since Hungary's political volte-face was only half-hearted it was not regarded as an ally by the invading Russians, and the Red Army moved in as conquerors, providing the population and the retreating Germans alike with a bitter foretaste of their upcoming defeat. There were many incidents of extreme brutality perpetrated against civilians by Russian soldiers, while the corpses of horribly tortured German soldiers became a routine sight.

Chapter 14

The hour of the marksman

It was a small village near Nyiregyhaza. The Russian tanks that had overrun it had already moved on, and an infantry company had taken up position there. When the mountain riflemen approached there was a short and violent fight, which the battle-hardened Landsers quickly won. After suffering heavy losses the remains of the Russian company withdrew. Cautiously occupying the village, the riflemen found that its inhabitants had hidden in the cellars of their homes. When they realized the Soviets had been driven out they emerged and approached the Germans lamenting loudly. Searching the houses the Germans discovered why. They found raped women and girls, and the shot and bayoneted bodies of relatives who had tried to stop the rapists. Sepp and two of his comrades found a distraught old man whom they could not calm down, who kept pointing at the entrance to some sort of cellar. They assumed that there must be enemy soldiers hidden there and immediately spread out and approached the building. When their repeated challenges brought no reaction one of the Landsers took a grenade from his belt and was about to throw it through the open door when the old man came forward and stopped him. Screaming in Hungarian and gesticulating wildly, he pushed the Landser into the room. He had hardly entered before he turned back again, his face green, and propping himself against the wall he started vomiting. Forewarned, Sepp and a comrade looked around the edge of the door. The sight before them made them gasp aloud and horror constricted their throats. In the room lay a woman who had been in the advanced stages of pregnancy, whose belly had been cut open while she was yet alive and the embryo torn out. She had bled to death. The almost full-grown foetus had been nailed to a rafter with a bayonet. They took the murdered child down, wrapped it in a tent square with its mother, and buried them in the garden.

Two days later the regiment advanced to within firing range of the small town of Nyiregyhaza. While II Battalion awaited the order to attack, Sepp used the time to explore his surroundings. After a few hours of sleep he disappeared into the protective darkness before dawn. After a short time he approached the first houses of a suburb. Carefully he crept through the gardens and the ruins of destroyed buildings. The suburb seemed deserted, though it was said to be occupied by the Russians. Meanwhile the sun was coming up, so he had to watch out for concealed observation posts. While he dashed from one piece of cover to the next he suddenly heard vehicles coming in his direction. It was by now half past seven in the morning and he should really be on his way back to his own lines, but he could not stop thinking about having nothing to report from his reconnaissance and still hoped to discover something worthwhile. Walking quickly he climbed up a mound of rubble and hid behind the roof ridge of the former house. He silently cleared himself a space that would provide a clear view ahead.

Below him lay a street of plundered shops and a restaurant. A small truck and three American Willies jeeps with the Soviet star on their bonnets came around the corner ahead and stopped in front of the restaurant. The soldiers jumped out of their vehicles, orders were shouted, and they divided up into small groups and went into the houses. Sepp felt fear rise within him, but the Russians ignored his heap of rubble and concentrated on the buildings that were still standing and had been clearly abandoned. The soldiers started plundering and soon all sorts of things to ease a soldier's life were collected around their vehicles: jars of fruit, vegetables, meat, a gramophone complete with records, candlesticks, pictures, and bottles of alcohol. Since they didn't find as much food or alcohol or as many valuables as they wanted their mood became more aggressive and they became wilfully destructive. Pieces of furniture flew out of windows; books and clothes behind them. The senior officer finally took care of the most rewarding target: the restaurant. Sepp heard loud voices inside the building followed by the shattering of glass and the sound of furniture being smashed. Suddenly there came the sound of a machine-pistol volley, and loud orders and anxious screams approached the open door. The soldiers had found the landlord and his wife in a hiding place and now pushed and kicked them into the street. Sepp estimated the landlord to be in his late fifties, his wife twenty years younger. Their curiosity aroused by the gunfire the other

Russians returned to the vehicles. Sepp counted twenty-three of them. They were arguing loudly about something. Obviously it was the woman. Suddenly the landlord, foreseeing what was about to happen, went for the nearest soldier, but he was knocked down by the blow of a rifle-butt in his back. Two soldiers then dragged him off and tied him to a streetlamp by his arms and neck. In the meantime other soldiers had laid the screaming woman across the bonnet of the first jeep. One held her arms while two others spread her legs. The officer, a first lieutenant, took precedence. He pulled a knife from his boots and, making several crude remarks that prompted the other Soviets to laugh cruelly, he cut and tore off her underwear. Then he dropped his trousers and accompanied by the yells of his comrades he penetrated her with hectic thrusts of his pelvis.

From his hiding place just 30m away Sepp looked on in a strange mixture of excitement and disgust. But his feelings quickly turned to utter loathing and helpless rage at what followed. In order of rank every single Russian proceeded to rape the helpless woman one after another as she lay motionless across the jeep until, milky and cloudy, their sperm ran down her legs and dripped from the mudguards. Her tied-up husband, damned to watch helplessly, remained silent, but the look in his eyes turned diabolic, bestial. It took almost an hour for the twenty-three of them to finish, and Sepp was unable to do anything: he was too close and would never have been able to move or get away without being seen. Glancing at his watch it suddenly came to him: the division was due to attack at 09:00, and it was already ten minutes past nine. That meant his comrades were already heading for their objective. He just had to wait until they got closer and then he would be able to rejoin them as they passed and avoid the risk of being shot at by his own troop. Luckily the softening-up artillery barrage was falling in another part of the town. Amazingly the Russians were not particularly perturbed by the distant gunfire. Almost calmly they packed their booty aboard their vehicles while the abused woman was still lying unconscious on the bonnet. But what came next curdled Sepp's blood. Some of the Soviets were standing around the woman arguing again, then two of them grabbed her legs and spread them while a third pulled a flare pistol from his holster, put a cartridge in it and rammed the barrel between her legs. With a moan she came to for a moment just before he pulled the trigger. Hissing, the red flare shot into her body and started to glow. Sepp had never before in his life heard such a scream, as liquid, red glowing lava poured from between her legs. Insane in pain she rolled from the bonnet and writhed screaming and trembling on the ground. It took her several terrible minutes to die. Sepp was paralyzed in horror, but the Russian soldiers seemed to enjoy the spectacle.

At this moment Sepp saw the first of his comrades creeping through the ruins about 200m away. If he shot at the Russians now, he thought, he could possibly hold out until the rest of the battalion came up. Seconds later the first of his lethal bullets fell among the murderous Soviets. But they were experienced soldiers. By the time Sepp had brought down two of them the rest had thrown themselves into cover and started to return fire with disturbing accuracy. He had to press down into the rubble to avoid being hit by their hail of bullets. But he had achieved his aim. His comrades advanced rapidly towards the source of the fire and a few minutes later a violent firefight broke out all round him.

Miraculously the Hungarian tied to the lamp-post survived the hail of bullets unhurt. When the riflemen freed him he stared at his dead wife and the fallen Russians with a manic expression on his face. He did not seem to perceive his surroundings and stood rooted to the spot with his arms hanging limply. Finally his eyes settled on one of the Russians who had only been wounded. With an apocalyptic scream the Hungarian's paralysis left him. He rushed into the restaurant and seconds later emerged with a meat-cleaver in his hands and hacked and hacked at the rapist's twitching and writhing body in a never-ending rage. Blood sprayed over him, but he didn't stop until he had cut the Russian's body into pieces. After that he dropped his weapon and ran to his wife's corpse, falling on his knees and hugging her to his breast. Without a word but convulsed by crying fits he rocked back and forth. None of the riflemen dared to approach him. They disappeared as quietly as they could and left the landlord with his grief.

On 3 November 1944 the division finally crossed the Theiss and took its place in the new front line. Heavy rain followed and the Theiss overflowed, so that the Russians were unable to follow them as closely as before, so for once the adverse conditions favoured the Germans. But the Wehrmacht's resources were now entirely used up, so effective long-term resistance was impossible. Consequently by the middle of November the division had withdrawn to the industrial town of Miskolc.

After fighting had raged on Hungarian soil for several weeks the country's political and military situation had become increasingly unstable. The capitulation and defection of entire Hungarian regiments ripped huge holes in the front line that could not be filled by the available German units. Highly dangerous strategic situations resulted and the fighting around Miskolc was rendered entirely unpredictable by the desertion of so many Hungarian units. The strategic emergencies that arose between one moment and the next compromised every suggested plan of defence. Commanders had to lead their units from the front line so that they could react immediately to unexpected situations.

With disastrous weather, temperatures fluctuating between minus 10° and 0°C, and continuous rain and snow, the riflemen were soaked and frozen. It didn't help that their positions around Miskolc consisted of a swampy morass full of water. Seven Russian divisions and a mechanized corps pressed against 3 GD, which could not resist their assault under the given circumstances. It therefore withdrew into the town and entrenched itself amongst the houses. From these relatively secure positions it managed to repel the Russian attacks, but to the left and right of the town they broke through. Despite the catastrophe of Stalingrad, OKH still held to Hitler's instructions that so-called 'fortress' cities must be held at all costs, but since the Wehrmacht was no longer capable of strengthening or re-provisioning such 'fortresses' the order to hold such a position always meant the destruction of the unit involved. The fear of receiving a 'fortress' order hung over unit commanders like a sword of Damocles.

The riflemen defended Miskolc for days. Sepp's duty was to protect the battalion combat headquarters in the front line, which the Russian mortars and artillery were targeting with amazing precision. Again and again a mortar shell would whistle down, and everyone would jump for cover. But eventually Sepp left diving for the next trench a split-second too late and the next shell exploded close by with an ear-splitting blast. Red-hot metal splinters buzzed around him. Just as he dived for cover he was sure he had felt Death breathing in his face, and a slight turn of his head at that moment saved his life, because a piece of shrapnel tore open his scalp on the right side of his forehead rather than ploughing into his skull as it would otherwise have done. Sepp nevertheless felt as if he had been hit by a cudgel and was thrown headlong into the trench, where he lay dazed for several minutes. When he recovered his senses he crawled from the trench covered in blood, unsure of the seriousness of his injury. He called for the medical orderly with a voice that was cracked in fear. He was luckier than thousands of other wounded men in that help arrived quickly. The medic inspected his wound routinely and calmed Sepp down. It was just a superficial flesh wound, his skull being intact except for a scratch. But Sepp's legs were like jelly as a result of shock and he had to lean on the medic as they went to the aid station. This time it was his turn to receive priority treatment. An assistant cleaned the wound and then, tugging the skin together without wasting time with anaesthetic, he sewed the wound with a needle and thread and bandaged it. Sepp was told to report for duty after an hour's rest. He had now been wounded three times, and on 27 October he was given a silver Wound Badge, an honour received with a bitter taste. In his case the injuries had been mere trifles, but tens of thousands of other men had paid for these little pieces of white tin with mutilation and lifelong pain.

The loss of experienced officers and NCOs reached dramatic proportions in these battles. Since no replacements were available the losses were made good by sergeants being placed in command of companies, while captains led battalions. Kloss, having been recently promoted to major, had to assume command of the whole regiment.

On 10 November, Kloss called his battalion chiefs to a meeting in his dugout, which was installed in an industrialist's elegant mansion. The installation of telephone communications was impossible in the chaos of ever-changing front lines and mobile command posts, and contact with divisional headquarters was by radio. This was problematic because the Russians were making every effort to locate the German radio stations and destroy them with artillery strikes. After the meeting Kloss intended to tour the front lines, so he had sent for Sepp, who had found himself a comfortable seat in a corner of the drawing room from which to observe the officers as they bent over their maps. Outside Russian shells were falling at a seemingly safe distance, though occasionally one of the officers ducked when a shell exploded a little too close. But of course, the daily routine of war had to some extent blunted their fear of such noises. In front of the house the regimental radio van was trying to get information from divisional headquarters.

By a lucky bit of direction finding or the sure hand of a talented gunner, the next Russian shell scored a direct hit on the radio van. The explosion blew in the last windows of the mansion, plaster fell from the ceiling, and splinters whizzed across the drawing room. Everybody threw themselves to the ground. Kloss had been standing with his back to the window. When it was blown in he fell to his knees, his helmet slipping over his forehead and his eyes almost popping out of his head. Then he fell forward onto the table and with a strange tremble slipped to the ground. Sepp immediately knew that Kloss had been hit. The dust was still in the air as Sepp jumped over to him. Kloss was lying on his face with a hole as big as a five-mark piece behind his right ear. From this a little blood was bubbling to run in a red trickle across his dust-covered neck and disappear beneath his collar. When he turned him over, Sepp found himself looking into empty, panic-widened eyes, which he closed carefully. Sepp had lost not only a benefactor and guardian angel, but also a valued and appreciated comrade. It was no use dwelling on the pointlessness of his death. They immediately buried him in the garden without comment. All that remained was a cross made of pickets, on which crookedly hung the helmet that had failed him when it mattered most.

With the death of Kloss Sepp had to return to his company, and with that he lost his access to the better-quality provisions available to battalion staff. His company chief was glad to get such a good marksman, of course, and only loaned him to the battalion for special tasks. But Sepp liked these occasional changes, because before he went off he received rations from his company, and then when he reported in at his destination he claimed not to have been fed and received another allocation of rations. On top of that, when he went back and forth he usually travelled by means of the supply wagon that went from unit to unit during the night, and if he got on well with the driver he usually got some additional delicacies from him.

On 1 December, 3 GD finally gave up Miskolc and withdrew to the Slovakian mountains. The whole Eastern Front was in a state of quickening collapse. The Wehrmacht was in a fight without fronts. Besides the unstoppable tidal wave of the Red Army there were partisans and nationalist rebels everywhere. Strategic planning was impossible. Every unit just fought to save its skin, to avoid getting caught by the Russians, and to get back to Reich territory. The partisan attacks in their rear were a particular strain, the strength of the partisan movement having in the meantime evolved from scattered guerrilla groups into organized military formations, advised by Russian officers and well armed with captured German and smuggled Russian weapons. Their activities were strategically and regionally coordinated to both support and take advantage of the Soviet offensives. There were partisan units as strong as battalions.

By the end of January GJR 144 had already retired to the Gran valley between the Slovakian and Lower Tatra Mountains, where what remained of the Sixth Army tried to stop the Russian advance one last time by strategic redeployment. Sepp's regiment was moved into the Waag valley between the High and Lower Tatra Mountains, near to the city of Rosenberg, where, surprisingly, it received some replacements. Among these were two new marksmen, young men without any experience who had come straight from basic training and a marksman's course to the front. These 18-year-olds had been ideologically brainwashed during their training and now they thirsted for action against the 'Bolshevist storm', to reap a 'bloody harvest' with their marksmen's guns. One of them was placed in Sepp's battalion.

The partisan attacks increased in frequency and fierceness all the time and the regiment got involved in complicated battles in which the distinction between combatants and civilians got very blurred. The consequence of this was further brutalization. German soldiers who fell into partisan hands were usually badly abused and tortured to death, and the riflemen took revenge by taking no prisoners during battles with the partisans. Especially demoralizing were attacks on their supply convoys and the loss of the urgently needed provisions, arms and ammunition that they carried, which were either destroyed or fell into the partisans' hands, increasing their fighting potential yet further. Supply convoys therefore needed special safeguarding.

One of the first tasks assigned to the battalion's new marksman was to accompany five wagons fetching ammunition and food for the battalion. Near a deserted village they were attacked by a small group of partisans. A violent firefight developed in which their attackers were driven back into the village, where they entrenched themselves in the houses. After recovering from his initial shock the young marksman proved to be a determined and practised fighter and shooter. Guided by an experienced lance corporal, he managed to shoot several of the partisans in their positions. The Landsers finally drove the enemy away, but some of the partisans managed to escape. When they searched the houses it turned out that there were women among the people who had been shot. Whether they were civilians or not wasn't clear, since they wore no uniforms or badges and whatever weapons they may have had had been taken by those who escaped.

Two days later the new marksman was involved in another

partisan ambush near a little sawmill. In the ensuing gun battle he lost contact with his comrades and then got stuck in a position from which there was no possibility of escape. The partisan group was too strong and the riflemen were forced to withdraw. Looking back they saw the marksman lift his rifle above his head in a token of surrender, and the partisans swarmed round him punching and kicking. The riflemen returned to their lines as fast as they could, and after reporting to the company commander the order was given to mount an instant counterstrike in the hope of rescuing the prisoner.

About an hour later Sepp was one of the detachment of twenty Landsers who approached the sawmill to find that the partisans were still there. They worked their way unseen to a position just 50m distant, and then Sepp opened fire, shooting a guard. Firing wildly, the partisans put up a ragged defence before, realizing that they were up against an experienced and superior enemy, they withdrew into a nearby wood. The greater part of the riflemen pursued them while Sepp went into the sawmill with three comrades.

They groped their way carefully through the semi-darkness within the building, aware all the time of a strange buzzing noise in the background. When one of the riflemen finally reached the saw room he returned after a minute or two with a white face. He was unable to speak and just kept stuttering 'Da, da, da,' pointing back the way he had come. With weapons at the ready Sepp and his other two comrades edged forward into the twilight and realized that the buzzing noise was a spinning saw blade. As their eyes slowly adjusted to the gloom a picture of horror gradually appeared before them, sufficient to send a shudder down the back of even the most experienced soldier.

On the saw table lay the lifeless torso of the young marksman. In his belly the saw blade was still turning, and had reached up to his navel. Beside the table were his arms and legs, cut into pieces. To prevent him from dying too quickly by bleeding to death the partisans had tied ligatures round his limbs before cutting them off. The saw itself was spattered with blood and bits of tissue. Gripped with wild rage at this act of utter savagery the three of them stormed out of the building to help their comrades, only to find that the fight was already won. Only one of the partisans had survived, and he was now about 350m away, running across an empty field towards the shelter of another wood. Sepp knelt down, sat upon the calf of his right leg, rested his left elbow on his upright left knee, wrapped the sling of his weapon around his shoulder and aimed. He took two, then three deep breaths, concentrated, and fired. A fraction of a second passed and then the fleeing partisan threw up his arms and fell forward. While a brave rifleman went back to fetch the young marksman's identity tags, Sepp went to make sure that his enemy was really dead. With satisfaction he discovered that he had hit him right between the shoulder blades.

There was no time to bury their tortured comrade. To be honest, nobody had the stomach to gather all the bits together. Everybody wanted to get away from the place as quickly as possible. When their captain came to write the obligatory letter to the dead man's family he reported that he had died in action instantly, from a shot through the chest. The real face of war is indescribable.

The division continued its retreat and crossed the border into Poland, taking up positions outside Bielitz (Bielsko-Biala), near Auschwitz. The Russian pressure slackened temporarily at this point, since the focus of their offensive was further south. The riflemen were nevertheless hit by daily nuisance attacks. The main fighting line held by Sepp's company was on the edge of a village. The school and the teacher's house with its stable were directly in the front line. The Russian lines were about 500m away, the perfect field of fire for a marksman. All Sepp had to do was find a good position. The loft of the teacher's house seemed ideal, so he removed the tiles in several places to make the hole he would actually shoot through less easily identifiable.

While he prepared his position he felt sure he could hear a child crying. The noise seemed to be coming from downstairs. He left his rifle and carefully went back down in the direction of the noise with his 08 pistol in his hand. He searched through the ground floor without finding anything, but as he stood undecided in the kitchen muffled voices came up through the floor. Discovering a hatch in the floor made of planks, he quietly left the kitchen and fetched two comrades. Once they were ready with their guns in firing position, Sepp stamped his foot on the hatch and called: 'Come out with raised hands!' In broken German, a voice replied: 'Don't shoot, here only woman and child.' The hatch opened and a woman of about 40 came out followed by another with a child in her arms. It turned out that it was the teacher with her mother and child. Even though the riflemen described the danger of their situation to the women, they refused to leave their house as long as the German soldiers were there, the reason being that there was a cow in the stable that they needed in order to feed the child. When they went to look at the animal they found that it had been hurt in its abdominal wall by a grenade fragment. Its intestines were bulging as big as a medicine ball as a result of the wound becoming infected. The poor creature stood in its stall listlessly. If the pain grew too great it let out a moo that sounded like a wheezing cry for help. It would have been better to release the animal from its suffering, but it had to be kept alive for as long as possible to provide milk. So the Landsers and civilians tried to make the best of the situation. The soldiers cared for the cow, and in exchange the women cooked and cared for them. Stable and house were connected by a trench, and they blasted a small hole in the cellar wall to reach the trench unseen.

During the day Sepp sat in the attic shooting at the enemy lines, his ears blocked with wax to protect them from the bang of his rifle, which was amplified to a deafening volume by the enclosed space. But as expected it didn't take long for the Soviets to localize the enemy marksman's probable hiding place. Since a sniper of their own was unlikely to be able to make out Sepp's exact position across so great a distance, the Soviets decided to solve the problem with something bigger.

On the morning of the third day a lorry drove up alongside a barn in the Russian front line and unlimbered an antitank gun. While three soldiers manoeuvred the little gun into position, others unloaded ammunition from the lorry and piled it up behind the barn. It was a calm and dry day, ideal conditions for distance shots. Sepp had built a good support and a firm seat behind it. He took the first Soviet gunner in his crosshairs and aimed above his head. The shot hit his stomach, and he folded up like a penknife. Even before he hit the ground Sepp had the next one in his sights. Another body hit. They had to be inexperienced soldiers, because it took them so long to recognize their danger. Instead of taking cover the third gunner decided to load one of his wounded comrades on his shoulder and try to get back to the barn, but fate overtook him even as he picked the wounded man up. Most of the others now became clever enough to stay under cover behind the house. It was more in hope than expectation that Sepp next tried to put a bullet through the 20cm hole in the antitank gun's splinter shield to hit its aiming optic. He was not sure if he had hit it or not, but he did not see an impact on the shield. At that the Russians who still remained at the front of the house became very active and all suddenly disappeared behind it. At the same time the motor of the lorry started up and the vehicle disappeared the way it had come. The antitank gun stood abandoned, surrounded by three corpses. For the rest of the day it was as if the Russian lines had been deserted. In the evening a comrade reported that according to an intercepted message the operation with the antitank gun had been abandoned because the gun was damaged. After hearing this Sepp was understandably rather proud of his shooting skills.

But the Russians retaliated the next day, when a Soviet marksman started shooting at everything that moved. His first victim was the older of the two women. When she left the trench shortly before it reached the stable a bullet hit her in the breast. Without a sound her knees gave way and she collapsed forward, dead. The explosive bullet had opened a fist-sized hole in her breast and torn her heart apart. It would have been suicide to try to recover her body during the day, but her daughter nevertheless had to be physically restrained from trying to reach her. Only the riflemen's desperate reminders that she had to stay alive to care for her child made her see sense. When night fell, however, they retrieved the body under cover of the darkness and immediately buried her. For the next few days everyone on both sides was careful not to expose themselves, and things went quiet. Even Sepp did not score any hits. The cow that was so important to the child finally collapsed and couldn't stand up any more, so the cook released it from its sufferings by a shot from his 08 pistol and took its carcass to the field kitchen.

A few days later a reconnaissance team reported that the Russian 4th Ukrainian Army was preparing itself for the decisive battle. 3 Gebirgsjäger Division was put on alert, because the Soviets were already sending out patrols and mounting company-strength surprise attacks in search of weak spots in the enemy's defences. The Germans regrouped and the riflemen were ordered to new positions. The teacher and her child went with them to the next village when they marched off.

On 2 March 1945 Sepp was sent for by battalion headquarters. This was nothing extraordinary in itself, since he always got new special missions this way, but this time he was awaited by a lieutenant from the regimental staff, who welcomed him with a warm smile and held out his hand. 'Congratulations, my dear Allerberger. It is an honour to me to award you the Führer's Marksman Badge. You have been so successful that you are being given all three ranks at the same time. May I have your right forearm, please?' Then, taking a safety pin, he attached the oval badge temporarily to his sleeve and handed him a certificate consisting of a simple sheet of typed paper with his name inserted in the appropriate blank space. Some trivialities and good wishes were exchanged, and then the officer turned back to the battalion commander and Sepp was dismissed. Despite being proud to have received this award Sepp realized that holding on to the certificate or the badge was very dangerous, so he immediately went to the post room and sent them home to his parents.

The Wehrmacht Marksman's Badge was one of the most exotic awards of World War Two. Though it had been introduced by official decree at the end of 1944, it was awarded very seldom, because hardly any marksmen survived long enough to achieve the prescribed number of confirmed hits. The consequent small demand and manufacturing difficulties meant that few of the badges and certificates were produced. The destruction of others by their recipients is another reason why so few survive today. Often they were not even available to be awarded to the troops. Many Marksman's Badges had to be awarded using improvised certificates, as Sepp's was, sometimes without an actual badge, which, it was promised, would be sent on later. But because the military situation was by now deteriorating daily this did not happen.

Meanwhile the Nazi propaganda machine tirelessly promised all sorts of wonder weapons to the army. The wish was genuine, but its fulfilment was wanting. If new weapons came at all, they came in very small quantities. Encouragement for the soldiers to demonstrate their military virtues became demands for willing self-sacrifice. In this context marksmen became particularly important to the 'hold-out' mentality of the propaganda writers. Their deeds were expounded in purple prose in the newspapers and their hit scores were lauded. Demeaning words such as 'sniper' and 'insidious' didn't feature. Instead the term 'marksman' became a synonym for devoted and selfless soldiers, described in the papers by such terms as 'hunters', 'predators' and 'intrepid lone fighters'. Of course, the propaganda machine needed pictures of its new heroes, and since the occasional snapshots taken by war reporters weren't enough they arranged special photo sessions.

Since the marksmen of 3 GD had again and again achieved outstanding things and two of them had been decorated with the gold

Marksman's Badge a news team was sent at the beginning of March to write a report about them and take some photographs. The pictures were taken on a sunny morning. The photographer instructed them to pose martially and pretend to be aiming their rifles: 'The enemy should reflect in the eye of the hunter!' There was a funny incident while the pictures were taken. One of the marksmen, named Fritz König, had to pose with his rifle leant against a tree while he drank water from a clear mountain stream. The picture had just been taken and König had just raised his head with water still dripping from his chin when a Landser walking past said with disgust: 'Ugh! You drink that water? Even though 30m upstream there's a dead Ivan lying in it rotting? Ugh, I feel sick just thinking about it.' They thought at first that their comrade was just making a bad joke, but they couldn't stop thinking about it so they went along the stream to check. And sure enough, after going about 30m they discovered that there really was a Russian rotting in the water. It took just seconds for König to throw up.

When they returned to the photographer a Wehrmacht war artist was sketching a marksman who had one of the little ZF 41 sights on his K98k. On seeing this, Josef Roth remarked: 'No point in painting that thing, you can't see anything through it.'

The visit by the news team was also an opportunity for some memento pictures to be taken – for instance, a new marksman who had just returned from his training course wanted a photograph taken of himself with his idol Sepp Allerberger. The marksmen's wishes were granted the next day, since the camera crew had a small photographic laboratory installed in their lorry. Sepp enclosed his own pictures in a letter to his parents the same day.

A few days later a German patrol brought in a Russian prisoner who told them about a company that was preparing to take a piece of unoccupied ground about 500m broad in II Battalion's area. A group of eighteen experienced riflemen was therefore sent to locate the position of the Soviets and secure the area until the regiment could plug the gap and remove its first-aid station out of the path of danger. Sepp was assigned to cover this group.

A soldier's chances of survival depended on a sixth sense about things that are about to happen. Sepp realized that his current assignment might turn out to be a suicide mission, so he went to the battalion weapons and equipment sergeant and swapped his K98k for the self-loading Model 43 that had been held back for him. He also took four additional magazines of B-cartridges, plus some more rounds in his pockets.

An Opel Blitz drove them to the threatened sector in the night. They sat in the back silent, every one of them lost in his own thoughts, because they knew what was about to come and what they had to do. When the truck stopped and the tailgate dropped they jumped out, fell in, and received their orders, then disappeared into the darkness and marched in the direction of daybreak.

Sepp walked beside them with his weapon at the ready. After an hour, as the first pale light of morning showed above the eastern horizon, they began to ascend a small hill. Suddenly white flares hissed in the sky and illuminated the entire area. Murderous machine-gun fire scythed into the line of riflemen and tore seven of them to the ground, among them their sergeant. Moaning and twitching they rolled about in agony. The riflemen returned fire immediately and managed to find cover behind a hillock, taking five of the wounded with them. The Russians jumped up from their positions and attacked immediately. Sepp had meanwhile found cover near the other two wounded men and remained unseen. This gave him the decisive element of surprise. He let the first two waves of Russians out of their holes, and then suddenly stood up and opened fire at a distance of about 50 to 80m in his well-tried and tested method: always at the enemy who got up last. To be sure of his hits and for maximum effect he fired at the torso, and the explosive bullets ate into the Russians' bellies, tearing apart the abdominal wall and the intestines. The Soviets were utterly surprised by this fire from the flank and obviously confused. His comrades had in the meantime regained their composure and opened up a well-aimed fire of their own. The Russian attack faltered. After ten shots the magazine of Sepp's self-loading gun was empty. In seconds he had inserted a new one and resumed firing. Every shot was a hit. The enemy's fire did not come anywhere near him before twenty Red Army soldiers were on the ground screaming. He used his third magazine. By this time the screams of the wounded had demoralized the storming party, and they aborted their attack and withdrew to their positions. Sepp jumped up, zigzagged to the two wounded riflemen and threw himself into cover alongside them. As if by a miracle he remained unhurt, but his dangerous sprint through the hail of Russian bullets had been in vain. He could not help his comrades. One of them was already dead and the sergeant, his chest riddled with bullets, was only able to mouth a foaming gargle before he too died a few minutes later.

Back in the safety of their positions the Russians now sprayed the area with small arms fire. Sepp was pinned down where he was, with little chance of escape. To protect himself from the enemy's bullets he pulled the two corpses together for cover and rested his rifle on the thigh of one. Now the hour of the marksman had come. While his comrades supported him with covering fire from behind, Sepp took the Soviets into his sights from a range of about 100m. With his first two shots he took off the heads of a machine-gun crew, while bullets hit the bodies of his dead comrades and made them twitch eerily. After that it was just like target practice. Every Russian head that appeared over the edge of a trench was shot. Within less than ten minutes another twenty-one Soviets were dead. Suddenly a light machine gun was thrown above the trench parapet and opened fire, while two other soldiers tried to flee, one of them, clearly wounded, being carried by the other. The machine gunner had already been thrown back into the trench by a headshot, dragging his weapon back behind the parapet as he fell so that its barrel fired on into the sky for several seconds until the magazine was empty. Then Sepp took the two refugees into his sights. When his shot hit a bag across the back of the man being carried there was a spectacular explosion that tore the two of them apart. Obviously the injured Soviet had been carrying an explosive charge.

The detonation signified the end of the fight and suddenly there was a deathly silence. Even the screams of the wounded Russians fell silent. Minutes went by, and then the Landsers rose from their positions and carefully advanced in the direction of the Russian trench. Nothing moved. The entire Russian company was dead. There were more than fifty bodies scattered over the battlefield and twenty-one more lay in their trenches with explosive bullets in their heads. The sides of the trench were spattered with bloody bits of brain and bone splinters. The burst heads looked like grimacing skulls from medieval paintings of Hell.

The loss of this company seemed to persuade the Russians that German resistance in this area remained strong, and they revised their attack plans and regrouped their forces. This respite provided the necessary time for the Gebirgsjäger to evacuate their endangered aid station. However, the repulse of the Russian attack did not lead to a shift in their focus of attention as might have been hoped, but rather to a dramatic strengthening of their offensive forces. The next Russian attack, mounted three days later, was supported by numerous marksmen who took bloody revenge for the previous skirmish. Sepp's group had meanwhile been reinforced, but the Russian snipers cut down the German officers and NCOs with unbelievable precision. Sepp and his inadequately armed comrades had no chance of stopping the repeated assaults, and he was only able to score a few hits from his carefully prepared positions. It was a wonder that he and a few other Landsers survived this attack at all before they withdrew at the last second.

The few survivors dived from cover to cover and defended themselves as well as they could, the precise and rapid fire of Sepp's self-loading Model 43 providing covering fire as they went. It was just as they were about to move again that they lost their last NCO, a sergeant and platoon-leader named Willi Hohn. He had just risen to give the signal to move when the bullet from a Russian marksman hit him behind his eyes and nose. His eyes popped out of their sockets like two balls. Blood and bone splinters splashed behind them. He fell to the ground as if struck by lightning, but seconds later he got up screaming: 'My eyes, aargh, I can't see!' The rifleman next to him threw him down again to save him from the Russian fire. With horror he found himself looking into a bloody skull with empty eye sockets. It was debatable if he was lucky that the marksman had not used an explosive bullet, since one of those would have killed the unfortunate sergeant. But as it was he had some hope of survival. In the meantime he could not stop screaming and thrashing around wildly. While Sepp fired the ammunition left in his gun, his comrades grabbed the injured man and dragged him away with them. He survived his injuries to become one of Germany's many disabled war veterans.

Chapter 15

Hero of the day

At the beginning of the war awards meant something and were presented in a dignified setting, but now that the Landsers were in an endless fight for survival awards were regarded by High Command simply as a way of strengthening morale. The resultant proliferation of awards robbed them of a large part of their meaning. Receiving another award just became part of everyday life. But a few days after the battles described above the lieutenant from the regimental staff sent for Sepp again. 'Herr Lance Corporal, you seem to be some kind of guy,' he said as Sepp came in. 'I'm proud to award you the Iron Cross First Class for your bravery during the tactical regrouping of the regiment and the evacuation of the first-aid station. I must tell you in confidence that your deeds have attracted attention at the highest divisional level. There's something brewing, so be prepared for a surprise.' This time Sepp was given a decorative printed document and the medal in its presentation case. Sepp immediately pinned the cross to his left breast pocket, ditched the case, and posted the document to his parents.

By his actions in the recent fighting Sepp had not only proved his extraordinary personal bravery, but by his actions had also won a temporary strategic advantage over the enemy. Usually he would have received no more than a German Cross in Gold for this deed – the highest bravery award given to other ranks in the Wehrmacht. But the commander of Army Group Centre, General Schörner (promoted to field marshal on 1 March 1945) was trying to raise the morale of his troops by the unorthodox awarding of medals. Consequently Sepp had been recommended for the Knight's Cross because of his deeds, which was usually only awarded to officers and senior NCOs for personal bravery and extraordinary achievements of strategic importance. The Knight's Cross was one of the very highest decorations of the Wehrmacht and was usually awarded at a special ceremony and was accompanied by special leave to be taken immediately after the presentation. But with the collapse of Germany's military infrastructure the value and significance of medals in the dying Reich had diminished, particularly since the criteria for receiving them had been absolutely undermined. Now, as the Landsers put it in their jocular but accurate way, it was a case of 'line up for the awards and bring your mess kit with you'. So the awarding of his Knight's Cross, which Sepp received at the same time as his comrade Josef Roth, was quite a simple affair.

On 20 April he and Roth were asked to come to corps headquarters. They were picked up by an amphibious VW and driven to Mönnighofen, a small town near Mährisch-Ostrau. The headquarters was in some kind of farm that looked as busy as a beehive. Runners and vehicles came and went, orders were being shouted, and there were staff officers everywhere. They seemed to be busily preparing for departure. Sepp and Josef, with their worn-out fatigues and hardened faces, felt like pigs on a sofa among the neatly uniformed staff men. 'It would do them good to lie with their arses in the shit,' grumbled Roth. 'I could show them the right places.' They stood there like lost souls until at last a soldier brought a tin with herring in tomato sauce for each of them, then a piece of bread and a mess canteen with coffee substitute. So their long wait was well spent filling their stomachs, a rare opportunity for the Landsers these days.

The hours passed and the two of them were sitting on the farmyard wall when there was suddenly a call from the building: 'Where are the men for the Knight's Cross?' A sergeant came out and called to them with barely concealed sarcasm: 'Are you the riflemen that shall be knighted? The colonel and his sword are ready for the solemn ritual.' Slowly they got up. 'A bit faster, guys, we have the big event ahead of us!' Minutes later they stood in a sort of entrance hall and a colonel with the red stripes of the general staff on his trousers came towards them with a folder in his hand, followed by a soldier with a camera. Sepp and Josef involuntarily stood to attention with their carbines at their backs. 'Stand easy, gentlemen,' the colonel addressed them jovially. 'Please excuse the makeshift nature of this solemn occasion, but I hope for your forgiveness bearing in mind the current circumstances. Actually the field marshal wanted to congratulate you personally, but unfortunately there is no time. So may I thank you in his name.' With that he opened the folder and read:

'Army Group Centre Headquarters, 20 April 1945.

'To Lance Corporal Sepp Allerberger!

'It is an honour for me to award you the Knight's Cross of the Iron Cross and a presentation hamper on behalf of the Führer on 20 April 1945. I have learned from the reports of your commanders that you have demonstrated outstanding soldierly conduct and extraordinary bravery. I wish you much luck and a safe homecoming.

'Heil Hitler!

'General Field Marshal Schörner.'

Then the same text was read again but with the name of Josef Roth in place of Sepp's.

Then the colonel waved to a soldier who presented two Knight's Crosses, which were actually altered Iron Crosses Second Class, on a folded tent square. The officer took the first one, approached Sepp, and asked: 'Did you wash your neck, Herr Lance Corporal?' When he saw Sepp's surprised face he added: 'Just kidding.' Then he put on their crosses and carried on in a fatherly tone: 'I am really proud to have soldiers like you in our corps. My congratulations and my personal acknowledgement. I hope you survive the coming ordeal and return safe to your families and civilian lives.' With that he shook their hands, while the photographer's flashbulbs illuminated the scene eerily. 'You will get your proper Knight's Cross later, when the situation is consolidated, in a real ceremony with a document signed by the Führer. But for now may I give you these letters from the field marshal. As a sign of his personal acknowledgement they contain his signed photograph. Likewise signed photographs of your divisional commander General Klatt.'

Both of them recognized the bitter undertone in the colonel's words. It was clear to all of them that the war was lost and that complete collapse was just ahead. 'For obvious reasons you will doubtless want to receive the gift box from the Führer right now.' With these words two soldiers each brought in an artillery ammunition box measuring about a metre in length, 50cm high and 30cm wide, full of luxuries. With the words: 'All the best, gentlemen,' the colonel turned around and disappeared through the next door. Meanwhile the photographer had returned. 'May I take another picture for the international press?' With that he got them into position and the flashbulbs flared twice more. Before the photographer went away Sepp asked him if he would send a copy directly to his parents at home. This he promised, and he actually did.

With that the ceremony was over. 'Where may we put the presentation boxes for our heroes?' one of the soldiers teased them. At that moment the jeep driver came in. 'I'll be driving you back to your people, so put the boxes into my car.' While the soldiers took the boxes out Sepp asked the driver for directions to the mail room so that he could post a letter home. Under the circumstances he wanted to send his Knight's Cross documents home as quickly as possible. He hoped that mail from Corps Headquarters would have the best chance of reaching his parents. As a precaution he used two envelopes. In one he put the signed pictures, and in the other the documents. As it turned out the photographs arrived safely, but the envelope containing the documents got lost.

With their provisional Knight's Crosses around their necks they drove back to their units, where their arrival was eagerly anticipated. Sepp had no trouble unloading his box from the jeep, as his comrades almost forced their help on him. Once they were in their dugout the lid was removed and they were confronted by tins of meat and fish, schnapps, a bottle of cognac, cigars, cigarettes, chocolate and cookies. In a spontaneous orgy the entire contents were consumed, though Sepp naturally got a larger share of the cookies and meat. As hero of the day he also kept the bottle of cognac and the cigars.

The press was taken in by propaganda, and it picked up on occasions like this immediately. So Sepp's deeds were worth more than a headline in the local paper of his home town, the *Mittenwalder Nachrichten*. The issue of 25 April 1945 bore the headline:

'Our Mountain Riflemen as Marksmen.

'Marksmen of a *Gebirgsjäger* regiment fighting defensive battles in the area of Teschen have achieved extraordinarily high shot results. The marksmen of the 2nd Company, Gebirgsjäger from the Berchtesgardenerland, shot eighty-three Bolshevists on 1 April. Lance Corporal Sepp Allerberger from Mittenwald, who belongs to another company, annihilated twenty-one Soviets on 2 April and reached a total number of 100 hits. Lance Corporal Hetzenauer from Brixen near Kitzbühl in Tyrol reported his 200th hit on 3 April. He is the division's most successful marksman.'

Chapter 16

The momentum of collapse

3 Gebirgsjäger Division stood with its back to the German frontier. The circle was about to close. The thousand-year Reich built on hubris alone folded like a house of cards after just twelve years. Germany was bled white. It had brought war upon the world and now its enemies were closing in from every side. The maxim of Hitler – 'Germany will win or die' – had led to increasing numbers of futile hold-out orders and sacrifices since Stalingrad. The more disastrous the situation became, the more Hitler's supporters in the police, the SS and the Wehrmacht were given a free hand. By repression and the mobilization of the country's last human resources they tried to stave off the inevitable downfall and destruction. But drumhead court martials, Hitler Youth, old men and untrained scratch units could not delay the catastrophe. General Schörner, a convinced National Socialist, was promoted to the rank of field marshal and finally to supreme command of the Wehrmacht because of his unflinching determination to mobilize all available forces and subject them to the severest discipline.

In reality there was nothing left with which to halt the increasing vortex of chaos. The momentum of the collapse had grown to such proportions that it could not be stopped. The Wehrmacht's logistical infrastructure and lines of communication and command collapsed like a burnt house. The populations of occupied territories rose up against the Germans in uncontrollable numbers, and acts of terror increased on both sides as the violent finale approached.

Patrols of policemen, military policemen and Waffen SS were formed in an attempt to restore military discipline and enforce order amid the general chaos. The result was indiscriminate brutality. After trials that lasted mere minutes soldiers without their papers were sentenced to death and immediately hanged or shot, despite the fact that in the turmoil of the closing months of the war no bureaucracy existed to provide substitute documents to men who had lost their papers in action. So German soldiers often met an unjust and violent end at the hands of their own comrades. Civilians were killed with even less consideration, even though they had followed individual units as helpers and servants throughout the war. Groundless suspicions of subversion or collaboration with the partisans resulted in innumerable death sentences being handed out by drumhead court martials.

Although death had become Sepp's everyday companion, one incident of this kind deeply affected him. Almost at the same time as he had arrived in Russia in the late summer of 1943 a young Ukrainian woman had become a follower of the Gebirgsjäger Regiment 144. Twenty-two years old, Olga was the mistress of an administration officer. In addition to warming his bed, she also performed useful tasks for the regimental staff, including acting as an interpreter. She was an uncomplicated, funny woman whose one ambition was to survive these disastrous times. In no way was she the sort to have anything to do with partisans. She was just happy to get away from the narrowness and regimentation of her village, and hoped to find herself a better life somewhere in the West when the war was over. The officer to whom Olga was attached was envied for his pretty girlfriend, and Sepp had also looked at her longingly on a few occasions.

Whether it was the result of a malicious report on some jealous soldier's part, or the arbitrariness of the Waffen SS patrol that picked her up outside the regiment's positions he never found out, but Sepp witnessed her capture and her execution just ten minutes later on the alleged charge of helping the partisans. An attempt by some of the riflemen to intercede on her behalf was in vain and they were warned off with threats of violence. It filled Sepp with helpless rage when he saw that the administrative officer, her lover, did not make a move to save her, despite her heart-rending supplication. It almost seemed as if he was happy to get rid of her. It was known that he was married and he was presumably fearful that his affair would become known beyond the troop if he made a fuss. So Olga was driven under a tree in the back of a truck alongside some men in civilian clothes. Then cables were tied around their necks and around a branch above them. Stunned, the pitiable girl stood there, silently weeping as she looked around for her lover, still hoping for intercession. But the fine Mister Officer had already elegantly pissed off and could not be found. When all the cables were fixed, an SS man in the back of the truck slapped the roof of the driver's cab with the palm of his hand and the lorry moved off. The cries of the condemned became choking and wheezing gasps as one by one they slipped off the back. Like worms on a fishhook their bodies writhed in a desperate struggle for life. Depending on exactly how the cable strangled them their tongues swelled from their mouths or their eyes seemed to burst. Olga's death throes lasted several minutes. While the SS men seemed to enjoy the spectacle, the riflemen turned away in disgust, muttering bitter recriminations. Sepp had to control himself not to lose his composure. Yet a few days later the incident had become just another episode, like so many others in this pointless war.

The regiment had by now fallen back near Mährisch-Ostrau, while the Soviet front had advanced to Brünn. In the meantime the Russians had begun fighting their way through the streets of Berlin. It was no longer possible to talk about resistance being under coordinated and effective command. Depending on its organization, equipment, experience and leadership the Wehrmacht disintegrated into more or less effective pockets of resistance. 3 Gebirgsjäger Division was among those that held together and continued to resist. But the end was near. Immense numbers of refugees were pushing westwards, blocking the roads and paths.

The riflemen fought on with whatever means remained at their disposal. It was one of the bitter ironies of these last few weeks of the war that weapons and equipment suddenly appeared at the front that the Landsers had only dreamt of before. A company of Waffen SS marksmen was sent up to support one of the last attacks for which the riflemen mobilized their forces. Sepp could not believe his eyes when he saw their equipment. They were wearing special hooded camouflage smocks over their uniforms, had a camouflage cover for their helmets, and even had a veil that could be fitted around the helmet to conceal the face. Their webbing was made of green material. Attached to it was a bayonet that could be fitted to the K98 carbine and a very practical tool set. Every one of them had a self-loading Model 43 with a 4x telescopic sight. Two were even equipped with the new fully automatic Sturmgewehr Model 44, fitted with the same telescopic sight as the semi-automatic weapons. But the troop consisted entirely of young guys of about sixteen years who had been called up only a few weeks earlier. After a two-week course they had been formed into the 'combative elite of the Wehrmacht', which would now throw itself against the enemy in wild determination and self-belief of their invincibility. A lieutenant in his early twenties was in charge of the forty-strong troop. Sepp recognized the obvious callousness of the officer, which left no doubt in his mind that the lives of his men meant very little to him. When they marched off and disappeared into the maelstrom Sepp could only think: 'Poor wretches!'

The division fought its way back to Olmütz. In the meantime the rumour factory was operating at full power. 'Berlin is occupied,' it was being said, 'the Führer is dead, Germany is about to surrender.' Despite this the division continued to resist bravely. Then on 8 May 1945 the Russians suddenly withdrew to their own positions and ceased firing. Enemy aircraft dropped huge quantities of printed broadsheets reporting Germany's unconditional surrender and calling on the Wehrmacht to put down its weapons and surrender. 3 GD's last commander, General Klatt, did not want to deliver his men up to the Russians, rightly fearing that they would be mistreated and meet with an uncertain fate. On the evening of 9 May the final order from Wehrmacht High Command reached the division via radio:

'The staff of all units on the south-east and eastern fronts have been ordered to cease fire. The rebellion of the Czechs in Böhmen and Mähren may hinder compliance with the terms of capitulation and our communications in this area. The High Command has not received reports from Combat Groups Löhr, Rendulic and Schörner… Arms were laid down at around midnight on all fronts. On the order of the Admiral [Dönitz] the Wehrmacht has ended the hopeless battle. The heroic struggle of almost six years is over. It brought us great victories, but also heavy defeats. In the end the Wehrmacht was defeated by overwhelming numerical superiority. The German soldier has dutifully achieved extraordinary things for his people, and remained loyal to his oath. The homeland has supported him to the very end with all its strength… Even the enemy cannot deny respect for the achievements and sacrifices of Germany's fighting men on land, at sea and in the air. Because of that every soldier can put down his weapon with dignity and pride… In this hour the Wehrmacht thinks of those comrades who fell. Our dead oblige us to continue in our unconditional loyalty, obedience and discipline towards the Fatherland, that is bleeding from uncounted wounds.'

The officers read this order to the miserable remnants of their battalions and companies. They looked into emaciated and hardened faces and an uncertain and often horrible future.

General Klatt decided to release all soldiers of the division from their oath and give them the chance to make their own way home. But this was easier said than done. As well as the uncounted holes in the German front line through which the Soviet units were pouring there was also the problem of the Czech insurrection to their rear. Despite the roads being blocked with refugees, most of the riflemen opted to try to reach the American lines along the Moldau river using whatever vehicles they could lay hands on. But Sepp suspected that he wouldn't escape Russian captivity that way and he decided to make his way to Austria with a comrade named Peter Gollup, who had only been with the unit for a few weeks. They would have to get across 250km of enemy-held territory, but Sepp had plenty of experience of using a compass and of getting around unseen. To minimize the risk of capture they had to do everything they could to avoid confrontation. This made long-distance weapons like Sepp's carbine with its telescopic sight superfluous. In addition it was clear that hanging on to his marksman's rifle would have placed him in serious danger if he was caught – the fate of captured soldiers identified as marksmen was well known. Reluctantly, therefore, he realized that he would have to destroy his weapon and depend instead on a pistol and MP40. He went to an assault gun that stood nearby, with many Landsers perched all over it ready to try to break through to the west. 'Wait a moment,' he said to the driver, who was looking out of his hatch. 'I want to put my carbine under your tracks so that it's really ruined.' He pushed the butt under the left track then stood up and waved to the driver. 'All right, you can start.' The motor roared into life and the tank lurched forward. Its tracks grasped the stock of the carbine. Wood splintered and metal screeched on metal. With a dull bang the lenses of the telescopic sight burst. Then the carbine completely disappeared beneath the tracks. Seconds later a scattering of smashed pieces appeared behind the tank. Though his weapon had been just a tool, it was still a tough moment for him.

With a handful of exceptions all German marksmen destroyed their weapons either at the end of the war or before they were captured, and for this reason original marksmen's rifles are extraordinarily rare today.

Staring regretfully down at all that was left of his rifle, Sepp was suddenly awoken from his reverie by a loudspeaker-like voice in his ear. 'Attention, attention – this is the voice of Pan-German

Broadcasting.' Sepp turned around. Next to him once again stood the bushy-moustached Viking. 'By means of his determined strategy the Führer has achieved his aim of uniting his eastern forces with those fighting in the west to create a powerful military formation. After tough struggles, these troops have managed to lead their Bolshevist enemies to the capital. Here the Führer will give them the decisive shot in the knee, supported by Reichs-idiot Himmler and Propaganda Snout Goebbels. Sieg Heil, we've had it.' Even in their current bleak situation, the obviously indestructible sergeant-major had clearly not lost his gallows-humour wit. Patting Sepp's back and nodding towards the crushed rifle, he added: 'Don't take it so hard, old guy. Now your chances of getting home intact are much better. And don't you follow the masses when you piss off. Well, enjoy the peace, if you make it.' And with that he turned around and disappeared into the undergrowth like a ghost.

Sepp and Peter prepared for their long march as well as they could, but despite their best efforts they could not get hold of any food. However, the entire landscape to left and right of the road was strewn with the belongings of refugees, discarded or left behind, and from this Sepp and his comrade gathered up odds and ends that they could carry easily and that they might be able to trade for food on the way: various pots, a coffee mill, and two pairs of elegant ladies' shoes – they decided to take the shoes because of the everlasting vanity of women!

Only a few German units surrendered as the Russians had demanded, most preferring to try to escape to the West. The Soviets therefore resumed their offensive on 10 May, mounting massive tank and air attacks on the mixed convoys of refugees and military units that filled the roads. Even the smallest groups were shot at by fighter aircraft. Sepp and his comrade therefore decided to march at night and hide during the day. On the second night, while they were still in the German-settled Sudetenland area, they found a lonely farm. A wan light came from one curtained window. By now they were very hungry, and they hoped that they might finally get some food from the farmer. Carefully, they crept up and tapped on the window. The curtain was pulled aside and a 50-year-old man appeared with a candle in his hand. Seeing the two soldiers, he opened the window and asked them in broken German what they wanted. Sepp immediately recognized that he was a Czech and instinctively stepped back into the darkness, but such was his hunger that his inexperienced comrade forgot his caution and offered to swap a pair of shoes for some food.

The Czech agreed to the exchange and took the shoes, saying: 'Russki soldier upstairs, shh. Wait, I back in few minutes.' With that he disappeared.

Though at the time he didn't know about the brutal expulsion of the Sudeten Germans by the Czech population, Sepp suddenly became very suspicious, because through the window he could see on the wall a framed German text and below it a German calendar for 1944. What was a Czech doing in a German's house? Why was a Russian soldier peacefully sleeping upstairs? He nudged Peter and whispered: 'Boy, this stinks! Forget the shoes and let's get away.' With that he pulled his comrade away from the window. But Peter said, 'No, I don't believe that,' and he extricated himself from Sepp's grasp. Sepp left him and ran back to the woods they had come from, hissing back at him: 'Come on now, stupid, before they get you.' His determination to flee unnerved Peter, who, after a last glance at the window, followed him. Sepp was 30m away and had already been swallowed up by the darkness, but his comrade had hardly gone 10m when the Czech reappeared at the window with an MP40 in his hands and opened fire. As soon as he saw the gun Peter sprinted for the woods. Sepp spun around at the first sound of firing and levelled his own machine pistol as his comrade hurried towards him. Then Peter fell as if struck by lightning, and Sepp opened fire. Glass shattered and the wooden window-frame splintered, and though he didn't hit the Czech he disappeared from the window and didn't fire again. Keeping low, Sepp ran to his comrade and dragged him to the safety of the edge of the wood, all the time expecting armed men to come out of the house. But everything remained deathly quiet. He let Peter down as soon as they reached the first bushes and turned him over onto his stomach. Peter moaned. Sepp felt the cloth of his uniform and found it was warm with blood. The Czech's volley had mortally wounded him. When he turned him onto his back again he was already unconscious, and after a few minutes he died.

Sepp had kept the corner of his eye on the house all this time, but there was still no sign of movement. He fled as soon as Peter died, orientating himself by means of the pole star and his small pocket compass. Now that he was on his own he had to be especially careful, since he had heard that the Czech partisans had taken to wearing German uniforms to lure their enemies out of hiding. Sepp therefore hid from small groups of men in German uniforms that marched past him, especially when he hid up during the day. As he was looking for a hiding place on the second day of his escape he suddenly heard German voices nearby. Creeping in their direction he saw a small group of men from his own division's artillery regiment. Carefully he called to them, and then rose from his hiding place. Before he could introduce himself one of them recognized him: 'It's Sepp Allerberger, the marksman with many kills to his name. He has the gold Marksman's Badge and the Knight's Cross.' The group consisted of twelve soldiers led by the regimental cook, a staff sergeant named Viermaier. Once Sepp's name was mentioned a debate broke out among them whether or not they should take him with them. The skill of the Nazi propaganda machine now worked against him, because there had been lots of newspaper articles about Germany's marksmen that described their achievements in glowing terms, and photographs had been printed of many of them. Sepp in particular had often been the subject of these stories. It was quite likely that the Czechs and Russians knew his name and what he looked like and would be watching out for him. So the majority of the Landsers feared heavy punishment if they should be caught with such an infamous marksman in their group. Sepp felt very uneasy about this and wanted to go his own way, but the staff sergeant finally put his foot down and stopped the discussion, saying that Sepp could come with them. But he always had to walk at the end of the line to safeguard their backs, and he crept along behind them for four days, doing as little as possible to remind them of his presence.

Feeling safe in such a large group, the Landsers continued to travel by day rather than under cover of darkness. On the fourth day they found a dead Czech. The blood on his chest was not dry yet, so he had to have died only shortly before they got there. Curious but uneasy, they stood around him speculating what could have happened. Then suddenly the body opened its eyes. His chest heaved and with a loud wheeze a glob of blood came out of his mouth. At the same moment he sat up, grabbed the MP40 that was lying next to him and pulled the trigger. The riflemen ran in all directions and threw themselves down in the grass. The bullets hissed high overhead without doing any harm, and mere seconds later the Czech fell down dead and the rest of his machine-pistol's magazine emptied into the sky. Now the riflemen were all on the alert, because it was unlikely that the partisan had been on his own.

At that moment three more Landsers suddenly called to them from about 50m away: 'Don't shoot, friends! We're riflemen from the 144th

Regiment, 3 Gebirgsjäger Division.' Sepp recognized them as soldiers from the regimental staff – one was the regiment's photographer, another its official war artist, and the third was a clerk named Schmidt, who was called 'Schmidtle' because of his smallness. The photographer was especially well known to Sepp, having documented many of his missions. The three of them had no fears of being with Sepp, in whose company they felt confident and safe, and Sepp was happy to escape the resentment of the artillerymen, so the four of them decided to part company with the latter. Since the photographer and Schmidtle both had compasses, Sepp swapped his with an artillerist named Thiermaier in exchange for half a tin of meat. After the incident with the dying Czech they were all anxious to get away as quickly as possible, so after the photographer had taken a farewell group photograph they wished each other well and parted. The artillerymen continued on their way in the sunshine while Sepp sought out a safe place in which he and his three new companions could hide for the night.

Not fifteen minutes had passed before they heard wild gunfire from somewhere quite close by. Sepp decided to reconnoitre the situation and carefully crept through the undergrowth in the direction of the sounds. After he had gone about a kilometre he saw the artillerymen involved in a violent firefight with some Czech partisans. Seven of the Landsers were lying on the ground, obviously dead. The whole situation looked hopeless. Sepp could see no chance of he and his three companions helping, since it would only have put their own lives at risk, so he returned to their hiding place. After describing what he had seen they all decided to look for a new hiding place and crept away.

For days they marched by night and hid during the day, always heading north-west. They avoided houses and villages and tried to avoid open roads and paths too. But they had one problem: the artist had been wounded in his right hand in an earlier skirmish with Czech partisans, and since it couldn't be properly treated the injury had become inflamed. He developed a mild fever and the wound turned septic after a few days and stank horribly: whenever they found water they tried to clean it and washed the bandage before putting it back on. They also had nothing left to eat, but they kept going by chewing birch leaves, sorrel and dandelion leaves and drinking their water mixed with saccharine pills, of which Schmidtle had a small supply.

As dawn was breaking on the fifteenth day of their march they looked for a hiding place on the banks of a clear stream. They were just tending their comrade's wound when they heard the sound of several vehicles. Sepp left the others and went to see what was causing it. After going about 500m he came to a road just in time to see four Mercedes trucks with SS registrations roll by. In their backs were unarmed Landsers. Instinctively Sepp ducked back into the protecting thicket. He guessed he must be in a section of territory still held by fanatical SS soldiers who hadn't accepted the end of the war and were still rounding up fleeing Landsers and subjecting them to their own brand of uncompromising justice.

At the onset of twilight he and his companions left their hiding place and continued carefully on their way. By their calculations they must be getting close to Reich territory by now. When they set out Sepp had reckoned that they had perhaps 250km to go, and allowing for their weakened condition and an average nightly march of about 15km at best he had calculated that it would take them about twenty nights to reach the frontier.

An hour later they came to a peaceful farmhouse. A woman was in the yard arranging her gardening tools. While the others hid in the grass the photographer went over and talked to her. Seconds later he excitedly waved to his comrades. 'We've made it, boys, we're almost home. We're more than 20km inside Austria. The Yanks have been here, but the Ivans are far enough away to kiss our arses.' Warm-heartedly, the woman welcomed them and asked them to come in, where she shared her food with them and cared for the photographer's hand. Besides potatoes and the first spring vegetables from her garden she offered them fresh yoghurt and apple juice. After months of privation this tasted like nectar and ambrosia. Feeling safe, they ate until they were fit to burst.

Like hundred of thousands of mothers, this farmer had paid for the bloody ideological struggle on the Eastern Front with the lives of her two sons. When she got out the clothes of her children for Sepp and his companions to change into, tears ran silently down her cheeks. The Landsers took the clothes gratefully. Then they washed and went to sleep in real beds, for the first time in more months than they could remember.

After having breakfast, again accompanied by yoghurt and apple juice, the farmer showed them the way they needed to go to reach the next village and they left, thanking her warmly as they went. She waved farewell after them, hardly managing to keep her composure.

Probably she was wondering why her sons could not have been among the soldiers returning home.

Rested and well fed, the riflemen felt reinvigorated. In high spirits, they marched in the daylight now and along the open road. They buried their weapons at the edge of a field, hoping that, being unarmed, they would be treated fairly if they should be captured by the Americans. They exchanged jokes and talked about their desires as they began to look forward to a peaceful civilian life. Then suddenly Schmidtle said: 'Boys, wait a moment. Our homecoming is about to get a fanfare. My backside is going to explode if I don't fart!' With that his face assumed a look of concentration, but instead of breaking wind there was a horrid squirting noise. His cheerful face suddenly froze to a mask of disgust and a foul smell came from his trousers. Clearly his digestive system hadn't taken kindly to its sudden reintroduction to such things as yoghurt and apple juice. His three companions could hardly stand for laughing as Schmidtle hopped about in his shitty pants. But his discomfiture at least taught them to resist the desire to fart themselves, which was a good job, since again and again throughout that day they had to interrupt their march and retire into the bushes. Schmidtle's organizational genius saved him from having to walk in his soiled underwear, for he had found several pairs of silk lace panties somewhere along the way to take home for his fiancée, and he decided to wear a pair of these while he washed his own in a stream and dried them. The photographer said: 'Don't sit anywhere near me if you want to take a shit while you're wearing those. If I see your naked bum and that sexy underwear I might forget myself!' They all laughed.

In the afternoon they reached the small village the farmer had described to them. Talking as they walked down to a main road, they suddenly froze at signs of movement ahead. Not 50m in front of them American soldiers were standing around a large number of captured Landsers. As they stood there for a moment hesitating between flight and giving themselves up, one of the American GIs spotted them. Unslinging what seemed to be a self-loading sniper rifle, he aimed it in their direction and called: 'Hands up, you guys! Don't move. The war is over, Krauts. Your bastard Hitler is dead. Your Scheiss-Führer can't help you any more. Come here. Keep your hands up, and move slowly.' Although all they understood for a moment was something about 'hands up' and 'Hitler' and 'Scheiss-Führer', Sepp knew better than to so much as twitch his lower lip. The GI could have shot them in seconds. Now, it seemed, the war had finally come to an end. Carefully they raised their hands and walked towards the GIs. While they were being frisked for weapons Sepp cast his professional eye over the American's sniper rifle. It was of technically sound and robust construction, but he was surprised to see that its telescopic sight was mounted to the right.

Another GI pushed them over to join the prisoners. 'Sit down there and hope for better times,' he said, smiling cynically. 'I think you'll be getting a long holiday in Russia.' The meaning of his words suddenly hit them. The war artist whispered: 'Damn, shit – they're going to hand us over to the Ivans. We gotta get away, or else we've had it.' At this moment a US jeep and two Mercedes trucks with SS registrations and driven by SS soldiers came along the road and stopped in front of the prisoners. The nearest Landsers were forced to get into the loading space and then they drove away again. 'Have a nice trip, you glorious Aryan heroes,' one of the GIs shouted after them. Now Sepp suddenly remembered the SS lorries he had seen two days earlier: they were conveying prisoners to the Russians.

Sepp looked around. Their guards were not too attentive, since most of the prisoners were exhausted and had resigned themselves to captivity. Clearly they didn't know about their extradition to Russia. Behind Sepp and his companions was a waist-high wall, and beyond that a bushy slope, a narrow valley bottom and then a thick forest – ideal cover for an escape. Carefully whispering to one another, they agreed that they had to get away before the next transport lorries arrived. While Sepp, the artist and the photographer were uncompromisingly ready to take the risk, Schmidtle at first hesitated, not believing that they would really be handed over to the Russians. But they agreed on the order in which they would attempt to slip away: the wounded artist first, then the photographer, then Schmidtle, and finally Sepp. The adrenaline shot into their veins, their hearts beat faster. Once more they were about to risk their lives in order to survive. When three trucks came into sight, they used the opportunity of the distraction to make their break. The artist and photographer disappeared over the wall unseen. But when Sepp called on Schmidtle to jump, he refused: 'Shit, I'm going to wait. I'm not risking my arse any more. The Yanks can't get away with delivering us up to the Ivans.' All Sepp's efforts to persuade him failed. The lorries were getting nearer and it was time to go if he was going to. Mere seconds were left. 'Don't come then, housewife,' he hissed at the clerk. 'We'll wait for you for half an hour at the edge of the forest.' Then Sepp jumped over the wall, just as the lorries' brakes screeched. Minutes later he met up with his other two comrades in the woods, but the half hour passed without Schmidtle appearing. He would eventually return from the Russian lead mines of Karaganda six years later, a sick and broken man.

Sepp and his companions marched on west. They still moved during the day, but now they took greater care because of the American patrols. On one occasion they took to an overgrown path to avoid a small village and got quite a turn when suddenly they were attacked by figures as thin as skeletons wearing striped suits. A violent brawl developed, but luckily their attackers were so weak that they were able to defend themselves from serious harm, standing back to back and punching at the starved bodies and faces. Even so, in the course of the mêlée their enemies' many hands stripped them of most of what they were carrying. Then, as suddenly as it had begun, the strange episode was over. Like wraiths, their attackers disappeared back into the bushes. The three comrades stood there out of breath and bewildered, seeking for an explanation for their strange assailants. They finally agreed that they must be the homeless inmates of a mental asylum. It was only some months later that Sepp realized they were the former inmates of a concentration camp who had escaped their guards and were plundering the neighbourhood. When he eventually learned the full horror of the German camps his feelings about the attack became a strange mixture of guilt and certainty in his right to defend himself.

The next day they reached the town of Linz, which seemed to consist of nothing but refugees. Here they managed to find themselves a place in the back of an overfilled Opel Blitz truck, but after travelling a few kilometres from the town their ride ended at an American roadblock. All the passengers were lined up along the edge of the road and searched – this time more carefully. Everything the Americans could use as souvenirs was kept. On the orders of an embittered NCO every man had to expose his chest so that the GIs could look under the right arm for the tattoo worn by SS members. Then they had to sit at the roadside and wait. For the rest of the day any men of military service age who came along were stopped and searched and ordered to join the others already waiting. In the evening the entire group, now numbering more than a hundred, was loaded aboard lorries and driven back to the railway station at Linz, where they were herded into cattle wagons and taken to a holding camp at Mauerkirchen the same night. Tens of thousands of former soldiers were forced to camp here in the open air. The Americans had meanwhile realized that it was obviously impossible to supply such a huge number, so just two days later they started to release those wounded men who were able to walk. Such was the confusion of the situation that Sepp and the photographer, who had pretended that they all came from the same village, were released with the wounded artist in order to look after him.

From Mauerkirchen they were taken by truck to Garmisch-Partenkirchen and unloaded at the railway station. They were free! Their lives belonged to them again, even if they didn't quite realize it at the time. Their first priority was to get the artist to a hospital, but once that was done they would set out for their own homes. They watched as an overcrowded train rolled out of the station with people sitting on the roof and standing on the running boards. Sepp stared. Sitting on top of the last wagon was the Viking! He was speechless as they recognized each other at exactly the same time. The Viking waved to him, then put his right hand to his cap – which surprisingly still boasted its edelweiss badge – and gave him a final military salutation. Instinctively Sepp did the same, and watched until the train disappeared out of sight. Sepp would never see the Viking again, but he has never forgotten him.

A few hours later he stood outside his parents' house in the small village near Mittenwald. The houses were as tranquil as if they had slept through the entire war. It was 5 June 1945. Sepp Allerberger had survived the inferno almost unhurt – physically. But his heart would remain hard and scarred for the rest of his life. The spectre of war would never let go of him.

Epilogue

Beyond the mountains the first light of a new day came up. Sepp came back from dark memories and found himself holding his right forefinger, which had brought death to so many enemies. He asked himself the same questions he had asked many times before. Was it right to do what he had done? Was there any alternative under the given circumstances? Was there any difference between his own fight for survival and those of the many enemies he had killed, who had been put in the same situation and subjected to the same grim laws of war? They were questions to which a lance corporal would never find the answers. Ordinary Landsers never had a choice. For them it was a simple matter of fight or die.

Sepp became suddenly aware of the morning coolness and went back to bed to get some sleep. As he lay there he thought of a poem he had found on the back of a report sheet, written by an anonymous comrade:

The men under the sign of the hawk,
They recognize each other by their faces.
They shake each other's hands.
They don't talk.

When others talk and brag
They grow hard and silent.
In their hearts turned to steel
The horror lives on.

The horror of uncounted deaths
When they screamed,
Their comrades in need,
When they put their hands up begging,
Reddened by their shed blood.

The horror in the roaring of grenades,
In the crashing salvoes,
When the earth convulses and groans,
Burning like judgement day.

They were lying in the throat of Hell.
They were soldiers,
Doing their duty.